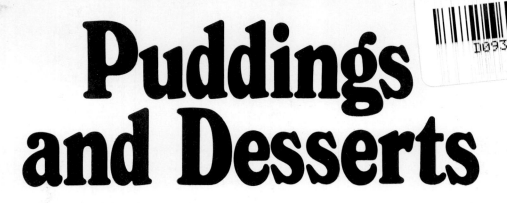

Puddings and Desserts

Puddings and Desserts

Elizabeth Pomeroy

Sundial

Contents

First published in 1977 by Sundial Books Limited
59 Grosvenor Street, London W1

© 1977 Hennerwood Publications Limited

ISBN 0 904230 42 2

Printed in England by Severn Valley Press Limited

Introduction

One of the many delightful things about puddings is that there is always one to meet any occasion – grand or homely; any weather – midwinter or midsummer; any person – hearty eater or choosy gourmet; any budget – large or small.

The British are renowned for the variety of their hot, hearty puddings, the French for gâteaux and rich pastries, the Italians for ice-creams and fresh fruit desserts. Which to choose?

First you have to consider whether it is to be a substantial part of the meal or a delicate finish.

If you are cooking for a family with the robust appetites of the energetic young, or adults engaged in strenuous work, one of the famous English hot puddings will be eaten with gusto and be both satisfying and inexpensive.

If you are having a party and the menu includes a rich main course, you need a light refreshing dessert to follow it – like Lemon Soufflé or Melon Sorbet. Alternatively you can plan the menu, say for a birthday, so that it builds up to the last course with a spectacular 'greedy' pudding such as Gâteau St Honoré or a splendid Baba, gleaming with Rum Syrup and filled with whipped cream and strawberries.

Some glamorous puddings which look

difficult are actually quite easy to make, like a Pavlova from Australia. Another mistaken idea is that hot puddings take too much time to make. In fact most of them are quick and easy to prepare and, once in the steamer, simmer away using very little heat and leaving one free for the next two or three hours to do other things. If you want to go out to shop, you can put the pudding in a deep pan or casserole in a low oven and it will look after itself. Another advantage in some families is that steamed puddings do not spoil if kept for late-comers.

For kitchen-dining room meals, there are delightful fried and pan-to-table puddings, ranging from Poor Knights of Windsor (one of the happier ways of using up surplus bread) or delicious little honeyed Greek Fritters, to the exciting rum-flamed Pineapple Pancakes from the Caribbean.

If you find yourself with an unexpected guest and want a last-minute sweet, you will find a selection under 'Quickies'.

Puddings are clearly making a come-back for a variety of reasons, not least economic, and not only give pleasure to family and friends but also provide fun and interest for the home cook.

All spoon measurements are level.

All recipes serve four unless otherwise stated.

Suet crust pastry

Metric	Imperial
225 g self-raising flour	8 oz self-raising flour
¼ teaspoon salt	¼ teaspoon salt
75–100 g shredded suet	3–4 oz shredded suet
Cold water to mix	Cold water to mix

Sieve the flour and salt together and rub in the suet lightly with the fingertips. Add just sufficient water to mix to a soft but not sticky dough, using a knife and your fingers. Turn on to a floured board and pat into a smooth ball. Use as required.

When a recipe says 225 g (8 oz) suet crust this means pastry which is made with 225 g (8 oz) flour plus the other ingredients.

Variation

If preferred 225 g (8 oz) plain flour with 2 teaspoons baking powder may be used instead of self-raising flour. 50 g (2 oz) of the flour may be replaced by 50 g (2 oz) of fresh white breadcrumbs which will give a lighter and more spongy crust. This is sometimes liable to break if the pudding is turned out of the basin.

Note : Suet is beef fat, easily obtainable already shredded in handy packs. It should be stored in dry, cold conditions. Should you find yourself with surplus fat on a beef joint, remove it raw and grate it rather finely, dipping the lump of suet frequently into flour so that it does not stick in the grater and the flakes remain separate. Don't grate it until about to use.

Shredded suet is used in two ways: in suet crust pastry or combined with flour and/or breadcrumbs in pudding mixtures. Both types can be steamed or baked, and are best eaten hot as the cooked dough becomes heavy when cold. Originally suet puddings were wrapped in a cloth and boiled but nowadays they are steamed as this gives the much lighter texture which is preferred.

Bramble and apple hat

Metric	Imperial
225 g suet crust	8 oz suet crust
450 g cooking apples	1 lb cooking apples
225 g blackberries	8 oz blackberries
2–3 × 15 ml spoons brown or white sugar	2–3 tablespoons brown or white sugar
75 ml cold water	3 fl oz cold water

Cooking Time: 3 hours

The combination of blackberry or bramble with apple is an old favourite, and never better than when inside a suet crust.

Grease a 1·2 l (2 pint) pudding basin. Roll out the suet crust into a circle about 6 mm (¼ in) thick. Cut out a quarter and line the basin (see opposite). Peel, core and slice the apples and fill the basin, layering the apples with blackberries and sugar. Gather the remaining suet crust into a ball and roll it out into a circle to put on top of the fruit. Damp the edge all round.

Trim the lining pastry neatly about 1·5 cm (½ in) above the lid, fold the edges over and press on to the lid. Cover the basin (see page 10) and steam the pudding (see page 10) for 3 hours. Lift out and allow to shrink slightly. Place a hot serving platter on top, invert the platter and basin together and unmould carefully. Serve hot with a bowl of brown sugar and custard or cream.

Baked roly-poly pudding

Metric	Imperial
225 g suet crust (see page 8)	8 oz suet crust (see page 8)
75–100 g warm jam	3–4 oz warm jam
Milk and sugar for glazing (optional)	Milk and sugar for glazing (optional)

Cooking Time: 30–40 minutes
Oven: 200°C, 400°F, Gas Mark 6

Roll out the suet crust about 6 mm ($\frac{1}{4}$ in) thick into a rectangle about 25 cm × 20 cm (10 in × 8 in). Spread evenly with warm jam leaving a border about 1·5 cm/$\frac{1}{2}$ in wide all round. Fold this border over the jam and brush with water. Roll up, not too tightly, from one of the shorter sides. Press the top edge down, seal it and press the ends together.

Turn roly-poly upside down on a piece of greased foil or greaseproof paper large enough to come halfway up the sides of the roll. Tie loosely about 5 cm (2 in) from each end, leaving room for the pastry to rise. Cut 4 slits across pastry top to allow the steam to escape. Brush lightly with milk and sprinkle with sugar; alternatively dredge with sugar after baking. Bake in a hot oven for 30–40 minutes until well risen and golden. Remove paper case and serve hot with cream or custard.

Variations

Steamed roly-poly

Cooking Time: 1$\frac{1}{2}$–2 hours

Prepare a saucepan of boiling water with steamer on top. Make the roly-poly as for baking, above. Turn it upside down on a sheet of greased foil large enough to wrap round it, leaving room for the pastry to rise. Seal the joins on top and at the ends by pleating or rolling them firmly together. Place in the steamer and cook for 1$\frac{1}{2}$–2 hours (see page 10). When cooked, open foil and roll pudding carefully on to a warm serving dish. Serve hot with custard or Jam Sauce (see page 14).

Mincemeat and syrup roly-poly
Spread suet crust with mincemeat and trickle over 2–3 × 15 ml spoons (2–3 tablespoons) golden syrup.

Baked apple dumplings

Metric	Imperial
225 suet crust	8 oz suet crust
4 medium apples	4 medium apples
4 × 5 ml heaped spoons brown sugar or mincemeat	4 heaped teaspoons brown sugar or mincemeat
1 egg white, beaten	1 egg white, beaten
4 × 5 ml spoons caster sugar	4 teaspoons caster sugar

Cooking Time: 30 minutes
Oven 200°C, 400°F, Gas Mark 6

Roll out the suet crust thinly into a square and cut into four equal pieces. Peel and core the apples and put one in the centre of each pastry square. Fill the apple centre with brown sugar or mincemeat. Brush the edge of each pastry square with water, draw the corners up to meet over the centre of each apple and press the edges firmly together. Decorate with pastry leaves. Put on a greased baking tin. Brush with egg white and sprinkle with sugar. Bake in a hot oven for 30 minutes. Serve hot with Rum Butter (see page 22).

Variation

Steamed apple dumplings
Prepare apples and wrap in suet crust as above. Place each dumpling upside down on a square of greased foil large enough to wrap loosely round it, allowing room for the pastry to rise. Place the dumplings in a steamer over a saucepan of boiling water and cook for 45–60 minutes. Serve hot with Apricot Jam Sauce (see page 14).

Steamed college pudding

Metric	Imperial
50 g self-raising flour	2 oz self-raising flour
50 g brown breadcrumbs	2 oz brown breadcrumbs
½ teaspoon mixed spice	½ teaspoon mixed spice
25 g brown sugar	1 oz brown sugar
50 g shredded suet	2 oz shredded suet
75 g mixed dried fruit	3 oz mixed dried fruit
(sultanas, raisins, currants)	(sultanas, raisins, currants)
25 g candied peel, chopped	1 oz candied peel, chopped
1 egg, beaten	1 egg, beaten
3–4 × 15 ml spoons milk	3–4 tablespoons milk

Cooking Time: 2–2½ hours

Grease a 900 ml (1½ pint) pudding basin and prepare a steamer. Mix together the dry ingredients. Mix in the beaten egg and enough milk to produce a soft consistency which drops easily from the spoon in 5 seconds. Turn into the basin, cover with greased foil and tie down securely. Steam for 2–2½ hours (see page 10). Remove from heat and allow to shrink slightly before turning out. Serve hot with Lemon Foam Sauce (see page 26) or Brandy Butter (see page 22).

Snowdon pudding

Metric	Imperial
100 g raisins	4 oz raisins
25 g glacé cherries, halved	1 oz glacé cherries, halved
100 g shredded suet	4 oz shredded suet
100 g breadcrumbs	4 oz breadcrumbs
25 g ground rice	1 oz ground rice
Finely grated rind of 1 lemon	Finely grated rind of 1 lemon
75 g lemon marmalade	3 oz lemon marmalade
2 eggs, beaten	2 eggs, beaten
3–4 × 15 ml spoons milk	3–4 tablespoons milk

Cooking Time: 1½–2 hours

This is a warming and satisfying Welsh pudding well suited to climbers or other hungry and energetic folk. Prepare a steamer and well grease a 1·2 l (2 pint) pudding mould. Decorate the mould with some of the raisins and the glacé cherries, cut side down. Mix together the rest of the raisins with the dry ingredients. Stir in the marmalade and eggs and add enough milk to make a soft dropping consistency. Spoon carefully into the pudding mould so as not to disarrange the cherries and raisins. Cover with greased foil and steam for 1½–2 hours (see page 10). Remove from heat and allow to shrink slightly before unmoulding. Serve hot with Sherry Foam Sauce (see page 26).

Orange marmalade pudding

Metric	Imperial
5 rounded × 15 ml spoons orange marmalade	5 rounded tablespoons orange marmalade
100 g plain flour	4 oz plain flour
Pinch of salt	Pinch of salt
1 × 5 ml spoon baking powder	1 teaspoon baking powder
100 g breadcrumbs	4 oz breadcrumbs
100 g shredded suet	4 oz shredded suet
Finely grated rind of 1 lemon	Finely grated rind of 1 lemon
50 g caster sugar	2 oz caster sugar
2 eggs, beaten	2 eggs, beaten
About 150 ml milk	¼ pint milk

Cooking Time: 1½–2 hours

This is an easy pudding to make and you can vary it by using different marmalades – lemon, grapefruit, lime or ginger. Serve it with a matching Marmalade Sauce. Grease a 900 ml (1½ pint) pudding basin. Spread 1 × 15 ml spoon (1 tablespoon) marmalade over the bottom. Prepare a steamer. Sieve together the flour, salt and baking powder. Mix in the breadcrumbs, suet, lemon rind and sugar. Stir in remaining marmalade and eggs and sufficient milk to give a soft dropping consistency. Turn into the basin, cover with greased foil and tie down tightly. Steam (see page 10) for 1½–2 hours. Remove from steamer and allow to shrink slightly before turning out. Serve hot with Orange Marmalade Sauce.

Marmalade sauce

Metric	Imperial
4 × 15 ml spoons marmalade	4 tablespoons marmalade
150 ml hot water	¼ pint hot water
1 × 5 ml spoon cornflour	1 teaspoon cornflour
2 × 15 ml spoons cold water	2 tablespoons cold water
Lemon juice to taste	Lemon juice to taste

Heat marmalade and hot water in a small pan. Mix cornflour to a smooth paste with the cold water. Draw pan from heat and blend in the cornflour mixture. Boil for 3 minutes and sharpen to taste with lemon juice.

Variation
Jam or syrup sauce
Follow recipe for Marmalade Sauce substituting jam or 3 × 15 ml spoons (3 tablespoons) syrup.

Steamed college pudding; Snowdon pudding; Orange marmalade pudding

Steamed cherry pudding

Metric	Imperial
175 g fresh cherries	6 oz fresh cherries
75 g brown or white breadcrumbs	3 oz brown or white breadcrumbs
3 × 15 ml spoons sugar	3 tablespoons sugar
Finely grated rind of ½ lemon	Finely grated rind of ½ lemon
300 ml single cream or evaporated milk	½ pint single cream or evaporated milk
2 eggs, separated	2 eggs, separated

For the cherry sauce:	For the cherry sauce:
100 g fresh cherries	4 oz fresh cherries
150 ml water	¼ pint water
40 g caster sugar	1½ oz caster sugar
Juice of ½ lemon	Juice of ½ lemon
2 × 5 ml spoons cornflour	2 teaspoons cornflour
1 × 15 ml spoon Cherry Brandy or Kirsch (optional)	1 tablespoon Cherry Brandy or Kirsch (optional)

Cooking Time: 1½ hours

You can make this pudding with either red or black cherries. The stones are quickly removed if you have a stoner; alternatively, open one end of a paper clip and use this to hook them out.

Remove stalks and stones from cherries. Mix with the breadcrumbs, sugar and lemon rind. Heat cream or evaporated milk, bring to the boil and pour over the mixture.

Whisk the egg whites until stiff, but not brittle. Beat the yolks with a fork and stir into the pudding mixture. Fold in the whites and turn into a well-buttered 600 ml (1 pint) bowl or pudding mould. Cover with greased foil and steam (see page 10) for 1½ hours until well risen and firm to the touch. Meanwhile make the Cherry Sauce. Remove stalks and stones from the cherries and put in a small saucepan with the water, sugar and lemon juice. Cover and simmer for 15 minutes. Mix the cornflour to a thin paste with 2 × 15 ml spoons (2 tablespoons) water and stir in 2 × 15 ml spoons (2 tablespoons) of the cherry liquid. Blend this mixture back into the saucepan and simmer, stirring well, for 2 minutes. Remove from heat and add the Cherry Brandy or Kirsch if using.

When the pudding is cooked, allow to shrink slightly before unmoulding on to a warm serving plate. Pour on the Cherry Sauce.

Rich chocolate pudding

Metric	Imperial
75 g plain chocolate	3 oz plain chocolate
50 g butter or margarine	2 oz butter or margarine
300 ml milk	½ pint milk
65 g caster sugar	2½ oz caster sugar
¼ teaspoon vanilla essence	¼ teaspoon vanilla essence
2 eggs, separated	2 eggs, separated
125 g fresh white breadcrumbs	5 oz fresh white breadcrumbs

Cooking Time: 1½–2 hours

Put the chocolate and butter in a bowl over a saucepan of hot water until melted. Remove from heat and stir until smooth. Warm the milk and add it gradually. Stir in the sugar. Add vanilla to the beaten egg yolks and stir into the chocolate. Mix in breadcrumbs. Whisk the egg whites until stiff but not brittle and fold into the mixture. Turn into a well-greased 900 ml (1½ pint) pudding mould. Cover closely with greased foil and steam (see page 10) for 1½–2 hours until well risen and springy to the touch. Allow to shrink before unmoulding. Serve hot with Chocolate Sauce (see page 74) or cold with cream.

Rich chocolate pudding; Steamed cherry pudding; Guards' pudding

Guards' pudding

Metric

175 g fresh breadcrumbs, white or brown
75 g caster sugar
2 eggs, beaten
75 g butter, melted
4 × 15 ml spoons raspberry jam
¼ teaspoon bicarbonate of soda
1 teaspoon water

Imperial

6 oz fresh breadcrumbs, white or brown
3 oz caster sugar
2 eggs, beaten
3 oz butter, melted
4 tablespoons raspberry jam
¼ teaspoon bicarbonate of soda
1 teaspoon water

Cooking Time: 2 hours

This steamed raspberry jam pudding was originally known as Burbridge Pudding and was perhaps adopted as a favourite by the Guards.

Mix the breadcrumbs and sugar well together. Stir in the eggs, the melted butter and jam. Dissolve the bicarbonate of soda in the water and stir thoroughly into the mixture. Turn into a well-greased 900 ml (1½ pint) pudding mould. Cover with greased foil and steam (see page 10) for 2 hours until set. Allow to shrink before unmoulding. Serve hot with custard or cream.

Queen of puddings

Metric	Imperial
75 g fresh white bread-crumbs	3 oz fresh white bread-crumbs
25 g granulated sugar	1 oz granulated sugar
2 × 5 ml spoons finely grated lemon rind	2 teaspoons finely grated lemon rind
25 g butter or margarine	1 oz butter or margarine
450 ml milk	¾ pint milk
2 eggs, separated	2 eggs, separated
2 × 15 ml spoons raspberry jam	2 tablespoons raspberry jam
50 g caster sugar	2 oz caster sugar
Sugar for dredging	Sugar for dredging
To decorate:	To decorate:
Glacé cherries	Glacé cherries
Angelica	Angelica

Cooking Time: 1 hour
Oven 160°C, 325°F, Gas Mark 3

Vary this old favourite by putting raspberries or black-berries in the bottom of the dish.

Mix together the breadcrumbs and granulated sugar. Add the lemon rind and butter to the milk and heat gently until the butter melts, then pour over the bread-crumbs. Stir well and leave to swell for 30 minutes. Beat the egg yolks and blend into the cooled mixture. Pour into a well-greased 900 ml (1½ pint) ovenproof dish. Bake in a preheated warm oven for 30 minutes or until firm and set. Warm the jam and spread over the pudding. Whisk the egg whites until stiff and dry. Sieve and fold in the caster sugar and pile on top of the pudding. Swirl or ruffle the top and dredge with sugar. Decorate with glacé cherries and angelica. Return the pudding to the oven and bake for 30 minutes or until crisp and golden. Serve hot or cold.

Friar's omelette

Metric	Imperial
3 large Bramley apples (about 700 g)	3 large Bramley apples (about 1½ lb)
Finely grated rind of 1 lemon	Finely grated rind of 1 lemon
Pinch of ground cloves or cinnamon	Pinch of ground cloves or cinnamon
50–75 g granulated sugar	2–3 oz granulated sugar
3 egg yolks, beaten	3 egg yolks, beaten
100 g white or brown breadcrumbs	4 oz white or brown breadcrumbs
75 g butter or margarine	3 oz butter or margarine

Cooking Time: 1 hour
Oven 190°C, 375°F, Gas Mark 5

Wipe and core the apples. Pour sufficient water into a roasting tin to cover the base thinly and put in the apples. Lay a sheet of well-buttered foil on top and bake in a moderately hot oven for 30 minutes or until tender; test with a skewer. Remove from oven and scrape out the pulp into a basin. Add the lemon rind, spice and sugar to taste. Beat in the egg yolks.

Well butter a 900 ml (1½ pint) pie dish or shallow casserole and spread a thick layer of breadcrumbs in the bottom. Pour over the apple mixture and cover with remaining crumbs. Dot all over with little knobs of butter or melt the butter and pour it over. Return to oven and bake for 30 minutes or until crisp and golden on top. Serve hot with cream or custard.

Bread and butter pudding

Metric	Imperial
6 slices white bread	6 slices white bread
50–75 g butter	2–3 oz butter
50 g sultanas, currants or mixed dried fruit	2 oz sultanas, currants or mixed dried fruit
40–50 g caster sugar	1½–2 oz caster sugar
2 large or 3 small eggs	2 large or 3 small eggs
600 ml milk	1 pint milk

Cooking Time: 45–60 minutes
Oven: 170°C, 325°F, Gas Mark 3

An agreeable way of using up surplus sliced bread is this quickly-made, ever-popular pudding.

Remove crusts from bread and spread thickly with butter. Cut each slice into four, either squares or triangles. Butter a 1·2 l (2 pint) ovenproof dish, preferably rect-angular. Arrange buttered bread over the bottom of the dish and sprinkle with fruit and sugar. Put in another layer of bread, the rest of the fruit and half the remaining sugar. Cover with remaining bread, butter side upper-most and sprinkle on the rest of the sugar. Beat the eggs well into the milk and pour over the pudding. Leave to stand for 30 minutes or so to allow the bread to absorb the milk. Bake in a warm oven for 45–60 minutes until set and the top is crisp and golden. Serve hot.

Friar's omelette; Bread and butter pudding; Queen of puddings

Summer pudding

Metric	Imperial
900 g mixed soft fruit	2 lb mixed soft fruit
100–175 g caster sugar	4–6 oz caster sugar
About ½ a sandwich loaf	About ½ a sandwich loaf

Cooking Time: 15–20 minutes

Aptly named, Summer Pudding contains a medley of any soft summer fruits available: raspberries, blackberries, red or blackcurrants and cherries.

Pick over the fruit, removing stalks and stones. This should leave 700 g (1½ lb) of prepared fruit. Put the fruit and sugar in a thick pan over very gentle heat and stir carefully from time to time until fruit is tender and juice has run. Cool and sweeten to taste.

Slice the bread fairly thinly – about 6 mm (¼ in) – and remove crusts. Line the bottom of a soufflé dish or 900 ml (1½ pint) pudding basin, cutting the bread to fit neatly together. Cut more slices in fingers to fit closely round the dish or basin, leaving no gaps. Half fill the dish with fruit, cover with sliced bread, add remaining fruit and cover closely with more bread. Spoon over remaining juice to soak the bread and just fill the dish. Reserve any surplus juice. Fit a small plate into the top of the dish, put on a 900 g (2 lb) weight and chill overnight.

To unmould, place serving dish on top of basin and invert both together quickly. Carefully lift off the basin. (Use a serving dish which will hold the juice when it runs out.) If there are any little white patches of bread, spoon over the reserved juice. Serve with cream, Devonshire if this is available.

Poor Knights of Windsor

Metric	Imperial
8 slices French bread, cut about 6 mm thick	8 slices French bread, cut about ¼ in thick
2 whole eggs or 4 yolks	2 whole eggs or 4 yolks
50 ml sweet sherry	2 fl oz sweet sherry
100 ml milk	4 fl oz milk
2 × 5 ml spoons caster sugar	2 teaspoons caster sugar
Butter or vegetable oil for frying	Butter or vegetable oil for frying
For the cinnamon sugar:	For the cinnamon sugar:
2 × 15 ml spoons caster sugar	2 tablespoons caster sugar
2 × 5 ml spoons ground cinnamon	2 teaspoons ground cinnamon

No-one seems to know how these little bread fritters got their curious English name. The original French recipe which came to England in the days of Agincourt was called *Pain Perdu* or *Lost Bread* and it is an excellent way to use up left over French or English bread, dinner rolls or brioches.

Remove the crusts from the bread and lay in a shallow dish. Beat together the eggs, sherry, milk and sugar. Clarify the butter by heating it in a saucepan until it stops bubbling. Remove from heat, allow to settle and strain it slowly through a fine sieve into the frying pan, leaving behind the sediment. This will stop the butter from browning too quickly. Alternatively, use vegetable oil, which does not need clarifying.

Reheat the fat until a piece of dry bread crisps quickly. Pour the egg mixture over the bread, leave a moment and turn over. Lift each slice out on a fish slice, allow surplus liquid to drip back into the dish, and slide bread into hot fat. Fry until golden underneath, turn and fry other side. Drain on soft paper.

Mix together the sugar and cinnamon, sprinkle thickly on each fritter and serve at once. Children may prefer warm jam or honey.

Variation

Fried jam sandwiches

Convert left over jam sandwiches into a treat for the next day by cutting off the crusts, dipping them in egg and milk and frying them like Poor Knights of Windsor.

Poor Knights of Windsor; Summer pudding

Scots Christmas pudding

Metric	Imperial
100 g plain flour	4 oz plain flour
Pinch of salt	Pinch of salt
1 × 5 ml spoon mixed spice	1 teaspoon mixed spice
½ teaspoon ground cinnamon	½ teaspoon ground cinnamon
¼ teaspoon ground nutmeg	¼ teaspoon ground nutmeg
100 g breadcrumbs	4 oz breadcrumbs
100 g brown sugar	4 oz brown sugar
100 g butter or margarine	4 oz butter or margarine
175 g sultanas	6 oz sultanas
225 g seedless raisins	8 oz seedless raisins
50 g candied mixed peel	2 oz candied mixed peel
1 dessert apple	1 dessert apple
50 g prunes	2 oz prunes
50 g golden syrup, warmed	2 oz golden syrup, warmed
Finely grated rind and juice of 1 small lemon	Finely grated rind and juice of 1 small lemon
2 eggs, beaten	2 eggs, beaten
65 ml whisky	2½ fl oz whisky

To finish:
Caster sugar for dredging
2 × 15 ml spoons whisky

To finish:
Caster sugar for dredging
2 tablespoons whisky

Cooking Time: 6 hours

This recipe produces a fruity, spicy pudding of rich dark colour, but, by using butter instead of suet the texture is less heavy and more acceptable to young children and many older people. You can use brandy or rum instead of whisky if you prefer.

Sieve flour, salt, mixed spice, ground cinnamon and nutmeg together into a large bowl. Mix in the breadcrumbs and sugar. Rub in the butter. Add sultanas, raisins and candied peel. Peel the apple and grate it down to the core, or chop finely, and add to mixture. Roll the prunes between your fingers to soften the flesh and snip them off the stone with scissors – quicker and easier than chopping. Add to the mixture and stir well.

Stir in the golden syrup, lemon rind and juice, eggs and whisky and mix thoroughly.

Turn into 2 greased 600 ml (1 pint) pudding basins or one basin double the size. Cover and steam (see page 10) for 6 hours until a rich dark colour.

To store

Lift out of steamer and remove covering to prevent condensation from the steam. When cold re-cover with clingfilm or buttered greaseproof paper. Wrap up in foil, seal carefully and store on a dry, cold shelf. If you want to store the pudding without the basin, allow to shrink slightly and unmould on a large square of buttered foil. When cold, wrap up neatly, sealing well. If you plan to give one of your puddings as a Christmas present, tie it up with scarlet or green ribbon and put a sprig of holly under the bow.

To reheat and serve

Reheat pudding in basin in steamer for 1½–2 hours according to size. Allow to shrink slightly and unmould on to a hot platter. Insert a holly sprig in top and dredge lightly with caster sugar. Heat 2 × 15 ml spoons (2 tablespoons) of whisky in a ladle, ignite and pour over pudding. Serve with Whisky or Brandy Butter.

Brandy, whisky or rum butter

Metric	Imperial
100 g unsalted butter	4 oz unsalted butter
2 × 5 ml spoons finely grated lemon or orange rind	2 teaspoons finely grated lemon or orange rind
100 g caster sugar	4 oz caster sugar
2–3 × 15 ml spoons brandy, whisky or rum	2–3 tablespoons brandy, whisky or rum

Traditionally served with Christmas pudding and mince pies, this is also called Hard Sauce because after it has been made it is chilled until hard and when served melts deliciously on the hot pudding.

Cream the butter with the grated rind. Add the sugar gradually, 1 × 15 ml spoon (1 tablespoon) at a time with 1 × 5 ml spoon (1 teaspoon) of brandy, whisky or rum on top of it. By adding the two together the sauce is less likely to curdle. Chill until required. It will keep several days in the refrigerator.

Scots Christmas pudding; Rum butter; Chantilly cream

Chantilly cream

Metric
150 ml double cream
2 × 15 ml spoons single cream
Few drops vanilla essence
2 × 5 ml spoons caster sugar

Imperial
¼ pint double cream
2 tablespoons single cream
Few drops vanilla essence
2 teaspoons caster sugar

Whisk the cream with a fork until it thickens, add the vanilla and sugar to taste and continue whisking until soft peaks form. Do not overbeat.

Variation

Fluffy whipped cream
Whisk 1 egg white until stiff but not dry and fold into Chantilly Cream. It 'stretches' the cream twice as far and is delicious served with both hot and cold puddings, hot chocolate and iced coffee.

23

Crispy pear charlotte; Brown Betty

Crispy pear charlotte

Metric	Imperial
450 g pears	1 lb pears
5 × 15 ml spoons brown sugar	5 tablespoons brown sugar
4 × 15 ml spoons apricot jam	4 tablespoons apricot jam
6 slices white bread	6 slices white bread
100 g butter, melted	4 oz butter, melted

Cooking Time: 30–40 minutes
Oven: 190°C, 375°F, Gas Mark 5

Make this attractive variation of the traditional Apple Charlotte when pears are plentiful.

Peel, core and slice the pears. Put half in a well-buttered 1·2 l (2 pint) ovenproof dish. Sprinkle with 2 × 15 ml spoons (2 tablespoons) sugar and spread with 2 × 15 ml spoons (2 tablespoons) jam. Cover with remaining pears, 2 × 15 ml spoons (2 tablespoons) sugar and jam.

Remove crusts from the bread and cut each slice into 4 triangles. Dip into melted butter and arrange on top of the pears, covering them completely. Sprinkle with remaining sugar. Bake in moderately hot oven for 30–40 minutes until crisp and golden. Serve hot with cream.

Brown Betty

Metric	Imperial
450 g rhubarb	1 lb rhubarb
100 g caster sugar	4 oz caster sugar
100 g fresh white bread-crumbs	4 oz fresh white bread-crumbs
Finely grated rind and juice of 1 orange	Finely grated rind and juice of 1 orange
75 g butter, melted	3 oz butter, melted

Cooking Time: 45 minutes
Oven: 190°C, 375°F, Gas Mark 5

The original recipe uses apples, but rhubarb, plums and gooseberries all make excellent Brown Betties.

Wipe the rhubarb and chop into 2·5 cm (1 in) lengths. Mix together the sugar, breadcrumbs and orange rind. Butter a 1·2 l (2 pint) ovenproof dish and fill with alternate layers of rhubarb and breadcrumbs; sprinkle each layer with melted butter. End with breadcrumbs and butter. Bake in a moderately hot oven for 45 minutes until crisp and golden. Serve hot with cream or custard.

Devonshire sponge flan

Metric	Imperial
100 g butter	4 oz butter
100 g caster sugar	4 oz caster sugar
2 eggs	2 eggs
100 g self-raising flour, sieved	4 oz self-raising flour, sieved
100 g apricot jam	4 oz apricot jam
25 g flaked almonds	1 oz flaked almonds
Juice of 1 orange	Juice of 1 orange
450 g ripe plums	1 lb ripe plums

To decorate:
150 ml double or clotted cream

To decorate:
¼ pint double or clotted cream

Cooking Time: 20 minutes
Oven: 180°C, 350°F, Gas Mark

Cream butter and sugar toget[her] light and fluffy. Whisk the eggs to creamed mixture, beating w[ell]. Fold in the flour quickly and lig[htly] into a well-greased 20 cm (8 in) sp[onge] in a preheated moderate oven for 2[0 minutes] until well risen and golden. Allow to shrink and tur[n] on to a wire rack. Heat the apricot jam and brush over the border and sides of flan case. Toast the almonds under the grill, spread on greaseproof paper and roll the flan in them until evenly coated. Spoon orange juice over the inside of the case.

Halve and stone the plums and arrange them overlapping in the flan. Reheat the apricot jam, thin slightly with water if necessary and spoon over fruit. Decorate with whipped cream or serve with a bowl of clotted cream.

Points to watch with sponge puddings
1. Soften the fat in a warm place before using but do not heat it, as it may oil and this makes a heavy mixture.
2. Beat the fat with the sugar until pale-coloured and fluffy in texture, using your hand or a wooden spoon. Do not leave an electric mixer running too long or the mixture will emulsify, producing a heavy sponge.
3. When beating eggs into the creamed mixture, add very little at a time and beat well between each addition. If the mixture starts to curdle, add a tablespoon of the measured flour each time egg is added. This is nearly always necessary when using an electric mixer.
4. Fold in the sieved flour quickly and lightly about a third at a time. Use a concave spatula; do not beat.
5. Usually extra liquid is needed to produce a soft dropping consistency – the mixture should drop off the wooden spoon by the time you count five.

Devonshire sponge flan

Orange sponge

Metric	Imperial
1 orange	*1 orange*
2 × 15 ml spoons golden syrup	*2 tablespoons golden syrup*
100 g butter or margarine	*4 oz butter or margarine*
100 g caster sugar	*4 oz caster sugar*
2 eggs	*2 eggs*
100 g plain flour	*4 oz plain flour*
2 × 5 ml spoons baking powder	*2 teaspoons baking powder*
1–2 × 15 ml spoons warm water	*1–2 tablespoons warm water*

Cooking Time: 1½ hours

This is the lightest of steamed puddings with a delightful fresh orange flavour.

Prepare a steamer saucepan and a greased 900 ml (1½ pint) pudding basin.

With a fine grater remove rind from the orange, avoiding the pith, then peel off all pith. Cut the orange into slices, on a plate so as to catch the juice. Spread the syrup over the bottom of the basin and arrange orange slices on it. Cream the butter and sugar until light and fluffy together with the grated rind. Whisk the eggs with a fork and add, a tablespoonful at a time, beating well between each addition. Should the mixture start to curdle, add a spoonful or two of the flour each time egg is added. Sieve the flour and baking powder together and fold quickly and lightly into the mixture. Add the orange juice and mix in a tablespoonful or so of warm water to produce a soft dropping consistency (it should fall off the wooden spoon by the time you count five).

Spoon the mixture into the basin on top of the orange slices. Cover with greased foil (see page 10) and put into a steamer. Cover and cook for 1½ hours or so until the pudding is set. To test, remove foil and insert a skewer; it should come out clean.

Remove pudding from pan and allow to shrink slightly before turning out on to a warm platter. Serve with Orange Foam Sauce or orange-flavoured custard.

Orange foam sauce

Metric	Imperial
25 g unsalted butter	*1 oz unsalted butter*
Finely grated rind and juice of 1 orange	*Finely grated rind and juice of 1 orange*
1 × 15 ml spoon plain flour	*1 tablespoon plain flour*
50 g caster sugar	*2 oz caster sugar*
1 egg, separated	*1 egg, separated*
Lemon juice to taste	*Lemon juice to taste*

Cream the butter with the orange rind. Mix the flour and sugar and beat into butter. Add water to the orange juice to make up to 150 ml (¼ pint). Add to beaten egg yolk and beat into mixture. Do not worry if it curdles; it will become smooth as it cooks.

Stir the sauce over gentle heat until it thickens and the flour is cooked. Just before serving, whisk egg white stiff but not dry and fold into sauce. Sharpen with lemon juice if liked.

Variations

Lemon foam sauce
Substitute lemon rind and juice for orange.

Sherry foam sauce
Substitute 50 ml (2 fl oz) sherry for lemon juice but do not omit grated lemon rind.

Raspberry lemon sauce pudding

Metric	Imperial
225 g raspberries	8 oz raspberries
25 g butter	1 oz butter
100 g caster sugar	4 oz caster sugar
Finely grated rind and juice of 1 large lemon	Finely grated rind and juice of 1 large lemon
150 ml milk	$\frac{1}{4}$ pint milk
2 eggs, separated	2 eggs, separated
25 g plain flour	1 oz plain flour

Cooking Time: 40–45 minutes
Oven: 190°C, 375°F, Gas Mark 5

An unusual pudding, this separates during cooking so that it has a light spongy top and a creamy lemon sauce on the raspberries underneath. Make it with any soft fruit or no fruit at all; it is still delicious.

Spread the raspberries over the base of a 600 ml (1 pint) soufflé dish.

Cream together the butter and 2 × 15 ml spoons (2 table-spoons) sugar with the lemon rind. Beat in the lemon juice. Whisk the milk into the egg yolks and beat very gradually into the creamed mixture, alternating with flour and remaining sugar until well blended. Whisk the egg whites until stiff but not brittle and fold into the lemon mixture.

Pour the pudding mixture over the raspberries and place the dish in a roasting tin with 2·5 cm (1 in) of water in the bottom. Cook for 40–45 minutes in a moderately hot preheated oven until the top is golden brown and set. Serve hot with a jug of single cream, or cold decorated with piped whipped cream and some fresh raspberries.

Fresh orange sponge with orange foam sauce; Raspberry lemon sauce pudding

Prune tutti frutti pudding

Metric	Imperial
75 g prunes	3 oz prunes
50 g glacé cherries	2 oz glacé cherries
50 g dried apricots	2 oz dried apricots
25 g angelica	1 oz angelica
100 g butter	4 oz butter
100 g caster sugar	4 oz caster sugar
Finely grated rind and juice of 1 lemon	Finely grated rind and juice of 1 lemon
2 eggs	2 eggs
75 g self-raising flour	3 oz self-raising flour
50 g fresh white bread-crumbs	2 oz fresh white bread-crumbs
2 × 15 ml spoons apricot jam	2 tablespoons apricot jam

Cooking Time: 1½–2 hours

The colourful fruit makes this light steamed sponge pudding look very attractive.

Select 3 large prunes and put in a saucepan with water to cover. Simmer for 10 minutes, then leave to soak.

Snip the flesh off the stones of the remaining prunes with scissors. Halve and set aside 3 large glacé cherries and chop the remainder. Chop the apricots and angelica. Prepare a steamer saucepan and well grease a 900 ml (1½ pint) pudding basin.

Cream the butter and sugar with the lemon rind until light and fluffy. Whisk the eggs and beat in a little at a time. Mix together the flour and breadcrumbs and fold in lightly. Add the lemon juice and fold in the chopped prunes, cherries, apricots and angelica.

Coat the bottom of the bowl with the apricot jam. Slit the plumped prunes in half, discard stones and arrange on the jam with the halved cherries. Carefully spoon in the pudding mixture.

Cover the bowl with greased foil (see page 10) and steam for 1½–2 hours. Test with a skewer, remove from heat and allow pudding to shrink slightly before unmoulding on to a warm platter. Serve with Apricot Jam Sauce (see page 14).

Almond and apricot pudding with apricot sauce

Metric	Imperial
50 g dried apricots	2 oz dried apricots
100 g sponge cake crumbs	4 oz sponge cake crumbs
50 g ground almonds	2 oz ground almonds
75 ml single cream or top of the milk	3 fl oz single cream or top of the milk
75 ml milk	3 fl oz milk
50 g butter or margarine	2 oz butter or margarine
50 g caster sugar	2 oz caster sugar
Finely grated rind of 1 lemon	Finely grated rind of 1 lemon
¼ teaspoon almond essence	¼ teaspoon almond essence
2 eggs, separated	2 eggs, separated

For the apricot sauce:

Metric	Imperial
25 g dried apricots, cooked	1 oz dried apricots, cooked
1 × 15 ml spoon cornflour	1 tablespoon cornflour
300 ml apricot liquor	½ pint apricot liquor
1–2 × 15 ml spoons caster sugar	1–2 tablespoons caster sugar
75 ml single cream	3 fl oz single cream
1–2 × 5 ml spoons lemon juice	1–2 teaspoons lemon juice

Cooking Time: 1¾–2 hours

Canned pineapple instead of apricots can be used for this featherlight pudding, and if you have trimmings from sponge finger biscuits left over from another dessert you can use them instead of cake crumbs.

Cover the apricots with 300 ml (½ pint) of water, bring to simmering point and cook gently until required.

Put the sponge cake crumbs and ground almonds into a bowl, pour over the cream and milk and leave to soak, stirring occasionally. Cream the butter and sugar with the lemon rind until light and fluffy. Add almond essence to the egg yolks; beat in, alternately with the crumb mixture. Drain, chop and add half the apricots. Whisk the egg whites until stiff but not brittle and fold into the mixture. Turn into a well-greased 900 ml (1½ pint) pudding mould and cover with well-greased kitchen foil (see page 10). Steam (see page 10) for 1¾–2 hours until well risen. Test with a skewer; it should come out clean. Leave to shrink slightly before unmoulding.

Serve hot with Apricot Sauce, made with remaining apricots.

To make the apricot sauce

Drain and sieve the apricots. Put the cornflour in a small saucepan and gradually blend in the measured apricot liquor and sugar. Bring to the simmer and cook, stirring, for 3 minutes. Cool slightly and gradually add cream. Sweeten to taste and flavour with lemon juice.

Almond and apricot pudding with apricot sauce; Prune tutti frutti pudding

Pineapple gâteau; Raspberry and cream swiss roll

Whisked sponge puddings
These light, quickly-made sponges are the basis of many desserts.

Points to watch
1. An electric mixer is speedy for whisking the eggs and sugar together, but the sieved flour must be folded in by hand, not beaten in by machine, if you want a really light texture. If whisking by hand, use a rotary or large balloon whisk.
2. The egg and sugar mixture is not ready until it falls off the whisk in ribbons which hold their shape on top of the mixture in the bowl for several seconds.
3. Use a concave spatula (see page 6) or large metal spoon to fold in the flour lightly and quickly.

How to line a swiss roll tin
1. Cut a rectangle of greaseproof paper or non-stick parchment 5 cm (2 in) larger all round than the tin. Grease the bottom of the tin to prevent the paper slipping about.
2. Lay the paper in the tin and using the handle of a metal spoon, press the paper into the angle all round the base of the tin, creasing it firmly.
3. Using scissors, snip the paper from each corner diagonally down to the corner of the tin. Overlap the cut points to fit neatly into the corners of the tin.
4. Brush the greaseproof paper with oil – this is not necessary if using non-stick parchment.

Sticky pear gingerbread

Sticky pear gingerbread

Metric

For the topping:
2 firm pears
8 glacé cherries
50 g unsalted butter
*2 × 15 ml spoons caster
sugar*

For the gingerbread:
100 g butter or margarine
175 g black treacle
50 g golden syrup
50 g soft brown sugar
150 ml milk
2 eggs, beaten
225 g plain flour
*2 × 5 ml spoons mixed
spice*
*2 × 5 ml spoons ground
ginger*
*1 × 5 ml spoon bicarbonate
of soda*

Imperial

For the topping:
2 firm pears
8 glacé cherries
2 oz unsalted butter
*2 tablespoons caster
sugar*

For the gingerbread:
4 oz butter or margarine
6 oz black treacle
2 oz golden syrup
2 oz soft brown sugar
¼ pint milk
2 eggs, beaten
8 oz plain flour
*2 teaspoons mixed
spice*
*2 teaspoons ground
ginger*
*1 teaspoon bicarbonate of
soda*

Cooking Time: 1½ hours
Oven: 150°C, 300°F, Gas Mark 2

This is an old-fashioned sticky gingerbread made by melting the butter and sugar instead of creaming them. It is turned out upside down to reveal slices of pear.
Well grease an 18–20 cm (7–8 in) cake tin. Peel, core and slice the pears evenly. Arrange the pear slices and the cherries on the base of the tin in a circle. Cream together the butter and caster sugar and spread over the pears.
Put the butter or margarine, treacle, syrup and brown sugar in a saucepan and heat gradually until melted. Add the milk, cool slightly and stir in the beaten eggs.
Sieve together the flour, spices and soda and blend in the egg mixture. Beat smooth and carefully pour over the pears. Bake on the middle shelf of a preheated cool oven for 1½ hours. Test with a skewer; it should come out clean. Allow to shrink before turning out upside down on a serving plate. Serve hot with custard or cold with cream.

Viennese caramel pudding

Viennese caramel pudding

Metric	Imperial
300 ml milk	½ pint milk
50 g granulated sugar	2 oz granulated sugar
50 g diced brown bread without crust	2 oz diced brown bread without crust
50 g sultanas	2 oz sultanas
50 g glacé cherries, quartered	2 oz glacé cherries, quartered
2 egg yolks	2 egg yolks
75 ml single cream	3 fl oz single cream
1–2 × 15 ml spoons sweet sherry	1–2 tablespoons sweet sherry
Lemon juice to taste	Lemon juice to taste
For the meringue:	**For the meringue:**
2 egg whites	2 egg whites
50 g caster sugar	2 oz caster sugar
To decorate:	**To decorate:**
3 glacé cherries, halved	3 glacé cherries, halved
12 small diamonds of angelica	12 small diamonds of angelica
Caster sugar	Caster sugar

Cooking Time: 50–60 minutes
Oven: 180°C, 350°F, Gas Mark 4

Put the milk to heat slowly. Meanwhile make the caramel. Spread the granulated sugar over the base of a thick saucepan, place over gentle heat and stir carefully until dissolved. Increase heat and boil briskly *without stirring*, until rich caramel colour. (If too pale it will not taste of toffee, if too dark it will be bitter.) Remove from heat and pour in about a cupful of milk very gradually, as it will bubble up fiercely. Return to heat and stir until caramel and milk are blended. Stir caramel mixture into remaining milk.

Mix together the diced bread, sultanas and cherries, pour over the caramel milk and leave for 20 minutes to swell. Stir in the beaten egg yolks, cream and sherry. Sharpen to taste with lemon juice. Pour into a greased ovenproof dish and bake in the centre of a preheated moderate oven for 30 minutes or until set.

Whisk the egg whites to a stiff snow and fold in the caster sugar. Pile on top of pudding, covering carefully. Ruffle or swirl top, decorate with cherries and angelica and sprinkle with sugar. Return to oven for 20 minutes or until crisp and golden. Serve hot or cold.

Note: White bread can be used instead of brown, or, for a sweeter pudding, diced sponge fingers.

Creamy chocolate mould

Metric	Imperial
40 g cornflour	1½ oz cornflour
4 × 15 ml spoons water	4 tablespoons water
1 large tin evaporated milk	1 large tin evaporated milk
75 g plain chocolate, grated	3 oz plain chocolate, grated
1–2 × 15 ml spoons caster sugar	1–2 tablespoons caster sugar

Cooking Time: 5–10 minutes

Mix the cornflour to a smooth paste with 4 tablespoons of cold water. Heat the evaporated milk, add the chocolate and gradually blend in the cornflour mixture. Bring to simmering point and cook, stirring, for 3 minutes until thickened. Remove from heat and sweeten to taste. Rinse a 600 ml (1 pint) mould with cold water, pour in the mixture and chill. Unmould on to a serving plate and surround with canned or stewed pears.

Note: The chocolate can be replaced by 2 × 15 ml spoons (2 tablespoons) cocoa plus ¼ teaspoon vanilla essence and the evaporated milk by 300 ml (½ pint) fresh milk plus an equal quantity of single cream.

Lockshen pudding

Metric	Imperial
225 g egg vermicelli	8 oz egg vermicelli
2 × 5 ml spoons salt	2 teaspoons salt
50 g butter	2 oz butter
50 g sultanas	2 oz sultanas
50 g candied peel, chopped	2 oz candied peel, chopped
50 g blanched almonds, cut into slivers	2 oz blanched almonds, cut into slivers
¼ teaspoon ground cinnamon	¼ teaspoon ground cinnamon
50 g caster sugar	2 oz caster sugar
2 eggs, beaten	2 eggs, beaten

Cooking Time: 30 minutes
Oven: 180°C, 350°F, Gas Mark 4

This simple and delicious pudding from Central Europe is traditional in Jewish homes at the Shavours Festival. Drop vermicelli into 2 l (3½ pints) of boiling water with 2 × 5 ml spoons (2 teaspoons) salt and cook uncovered for about 5 minutes or until just tender, stirring occasionally. Pour the vermicelli into a colander and drain well. Cut the butter into small pieces. Return the drained vermicelli to the pan. Add the butter and stir gently until melted. Mix in the sultanas, candied peel, half the almonds and the cinnamon blended with the sugar. Add the beaten eggs and mix well.

Pour into a buttered ovenproof dish and scatter over the remaining almonds. Bake in a preheated moderate oven for 30 minutes or until set and crisp on top. Serve hot with cream.

Sago cream

Metric	Imperial
600 ml milk	1 pint milk
40 g small sago	1½ oz small sago
¼ teaspoon vanilla essence	¼ teaspoon vanilla essence
50 g granulated sugar	2 oz granulated sugar
75 ml whipping cream	3 fl oz whipping cream
1 egg white	1 egg white
½ teaspoon grated nutmeg	½ teaspoon grated nutmeg

Cooking Time: 20 minutes

Heat the milk in a saucepan, sprinkle on the sago and cook over gentle heat, stirring frequently, for about 20 minutes until sago is soft. Add vanilla, sweeten to taste and pour into a bowl to cool.

Whip the cream until thickened, then the egg white until stiff but not brittle. Fold them together lightly and then into the sago. Turn into a pudding dish or 4 individual bowls or glasses. Sprinkle with nutmeg. Serve cold with Raspberry Jam Sauce (see page 14).

Note: This pudding can also be made with semolina, seed or flaked tapioca. If using whole rice, cook 10 minutes longer.

Spiced semolina

Metric

600 ml milk
40 g semolina
90 g caster sugar
2 × 5 ml spoons mixed
spice
Finely grated rind of ½
lemon
50 g sultanas
2 eggs, separated

Imperial

1 pint milk
1½ oz semolina
3½ oz caster sugar
2 teaspoons mixed
spice
Finely grated rind of ½
lemon
2 oz sultanas
2 eggs, separated

Cooking Time: 20 minutes
Oven: 190°C, 375°F, Gas Mark 5

Heat the milk in a saucepan and sprinkle on the semolina. Bring to the boil, stirring constantly, and cook for a few minutes until the consistency of porridge.
Remove the pan from the heat, stir in 2 × 15 ml spoons (2 tablespoons) of sugar, the spice, lemon rind and sultanas. Beat the egg yolks with a fork and stir into them 2 × 15 ml spoons (2 tablespoons) of the cooked semolina. Blend this mixture into the pudding and pour into a greased ovenproof dish.
Whisk the egg whites to a stiff snow and fold in the remaining sugar, reserving a tablespoonful for sprinkling on top. Pile the meringue on the pudding, covering it completely. Swirl or ruffle the top and sprinkle with sugar. Bake on the second shelf of a preheated moderately hot oven for 20 minutes until crisp and golden.

Floating islands with bananas

Metric

For the meringues:
2 egg whites
50 g caster sugar

For the custard:
600 ml milk
2 egg yolks
50 g granulated sugar
1 × 15 ml spoon cornflour
¼ teaspoon vanilla essence
2 bananas
2 × 15 ml spoons lemon
juice
25 g flaked chocolate

Imperial

For the meringues:
2 egg whites
2 oz caster sugar

For the custard:
1 pint milk
2 egg yolks
2 oz granulated sugar
1 tablespoon cornflour
¼ teaspoon vanilla essence
2 bananas
2 tablespoons lemon
juice
1 oz flaked chocolate

Cooking Time: 30 minutes

Heat the milk for the custard in a wide pan. Whisk egg whites until stiff and dry. Sieve in half the caster sugar and whisk again until stiff and glossy. Fold in remaining sugar. Scoop up meringue mixture in tablespoons and poach in the hot milk; simmer about 5 minutes until set. Lift out with a draining spoon on to cooking parchment or oiled greaseproof paper to drain.
Beat egg yolks and sugar together until pale lemon colour and blend in cornflour. Gradually mix in the hot milk left from cooking meringues. Pour mixture back into the milk pan and stir over very gentle heat until thickened; do not boil. Add vanilla essence. Slice bananas over the base of a serving bowl, sprinkle with lemon juice and cover with custard. Sprinkle with sugar to prevent a skin forming. Arrange meringues on top and sprinkle them with flaked chocolate. Serve cold.

Orange caramel cream

Metric

For the caramel:
100 g caster sugar
3 × 15 ml spoons water

For the orange custard:
Finely grated rind of 1
orange
300 ml fresh or frozen
orange juice
3 eggs
40 g caster sugar

Imperial

For the caramel:
4 oz caster sugar
3 tablespoons water

For the orange custard:
Finely grated rind of 1
orange
½ pint fresh or frozen
orange juice
3 eggs
1½ oz caster sugar

Cooking Time: 1 hour
Oven: 180°C, 350°F, Gas Mark 4

Infuse the orange rind in the juice over very gentle heat. Warm 4 × 100 ml (4 oz) dariole moulds in the oven so that the caramel does not set too quickly.
Put the sugar and water into a thick saucepan and stir over gentle heat until dissolved into clear syrup. Boil briskly, *without stirring* until rich caramel colour. Divide between moulds, and using thick oven gloves as the tins get burning hot, revolve moulds so that each is evenly coated. Work quickly before caramel hardens.
Beat eggs and sugar together until light and fluffy. Strain in hot orange juice, mixing well. Pour into prepared moulds and put them in a baking tin with 2·5 cm (1 in) of water. Cover with greased paper and cook in a preheated moderate oven until set and firm. Chill thoroughly. Unmould into individual dishes; the melted caramel will run down as a delicious sauce.

Floating islands with bananas; Spiced semolina; Orange caramel cream

Pancake batter

Metric	Imperial
125 g plain flour	4 oz plain flour
¼ teaspoon salt	¼ teaspoon salt
1 egg	1 egg
300 ml milk	½ pint milk

This should be the consistency of thin cream – you cannot make delicate thin pancakes with a thick batter. Sieve flour and salt into a mixing bowl. Make a well in the centre and drop in the egg. Gradually add half the milk, stirring with a wooden spoon from the centre and drawing in flour from the sides by degrees. Beat with a rotary whisk to ensure the batter is free from lumps and well aerated. Whisk in remaining milk. Leave to stand for 20 minutes or longer. This allows flour to swell gradually into the liquid before cooking and produces a smoother, lighter batter. Whisk again before using.

To make pancakes

300 ml (½ pint) of pancake batter will make 10–12 pancakes according to size, preferably about 18 cm (7 in). Use a thick pan reserved for omelettes and pancakes as it should not be washed, but wiped clean with kitchen paper or a damp cloth.

Whisk up the batter and pour it into a jug. Heat the pan and grease it lightly. An old-fashioned and very easy way is to rub it with a piece of suet held on a fork; alternatively brush with vegetable oil. Pour off any surplus fat because it will merge with the batter and make the pancakes heavy.

Heat the pan until the fat hazes. Lift it off the burner and pour in just sufficient batter to cover the base of the pan very thinly. Twist and tilt the pan so the batter spreads out evenly. Replace on heat and cook quickly until the pancake bubbles all over and is golden underneath.

Slip a palette knife underneath, flip the pancake over and cook other side. If it lands a little to one side, do not poke it with a knife as it will tear – shake it back into place. When cooked, flick the pancakes out of the pan upside down as the first side cooked should be the outside when it is rolled or folded. Leave the pancakes flat with a piece of greaseproof paper between each if they are to be stored in the refrigerator. If to be frozen, wrap the pile of pancakes in clingfilm or foil.

Variations

Lemon pancakes

A perennial favourite with both the family and the cook because it is so quick and simple.

As each pancake is cooked, tip it upside down on a sheet of greaseproof paper dredged with caster sugar. Sprinkle with lemon juice, lift the nearest edge of the paper and roll the pancake up. Serve at once.

Caribbean pineapple pancakes

Make 2 thin pancakes for each person. Fill each one with 2 × 15 ml spoons (2 tablespoons) heated chopped pineapple, fresh or canned, and sprinkle with demerara sugar. Place 2 filled pancakes on each serving plate and dredge generously with caster sugar. Heat a metal skewer and press it in criss-cross pattern on to the sugar which will caramelise in a lattice design. Pour over a spoonful of flaming rum and serve at once.

Normandy pancakes; Lemon pancakes; Caribbean pineapple pancakes

Normandy pancakes

Metric	Imperial
4 medium Bramley apples	4 medium Bramley apples
50 g unsalted butter	2 oz unsalted butter
50 g soft brown or caster sugar	2 oz soft brown or caster sugar
8 thin pancakes	8 thin pancakes

For the sauce:	For the sauce:
50 g unsalted butter	2 oz unsalted butter
50 g caster sugar	2 oz caster sugar
150 ml cider	$\frac{1}{4}$ pint cider

To serve:	To serve:
2 × 15 ml spoons Calvados or brandy	2 tablespoons Calvados or brandy

Cooking Time: 20 minutes
Oven: 190°C, 375°F, Gas Mark 5

Delicious apple-stuffed pancakes can be prepared in advance and put in the oven. Calvados (apple brandy) is sold in minature bottles; if unobtainable use brandy.

Peel, core and cut apples into short slices. Fry in melted butter until just coloured. Spoon fried apples down the centre of each pancake and sprinkle with sugar. Fold over the sides of each pancake and arrange them in a buttered oven dish.

Melt butter and sugar over a moderate heat, add cider and boil briskly for 3–4 minutes. Pour over stuffed pancakes. Bake in moderately hot oven for 20 minutes or until heated through.

Warm Calvados or brandy in a ladle, tilt sideways into a gas flame or use a taper to ignite and pour over pancakes. Serve while flaming. Allow 2 pancakes per helping and hand cream separately.

Crêpes Suzette

Metric	Imperial
100 g unsalted butter	*4 oz unsalted butter*
Finely grated rind and juice of 1 orange	*Finely grated rind and juice of 1 orange*
100 g caster sugar	*4 oz caster sugar*
8 thin pancakes (see page 40)	*8 thin pancakes (see page 40)*
2 × 15 ml spoons Orange Curaçao, Cointreau or Grand Marnier	*2 tablespoons Orange Curaçao, Cointreau or Grand Marnier*
2 × 15 ml spoons brandy	*2 tablespoons brandy*

Thin lacy pancakes flamed in an orange liqueur sauce are a favourite choice when dining out, but they can be happily accomplished at home by the host or hostess cook who follows this method, as the pancakes and the Suzette Butter can be prepared in advance.

Cream the butter with the orange rind. Add the sugar, a tablespoonful at a time, pouring a little orange juice on the butter, and beat both in together to prevent the liquid separating from the fat. Stop adding juice when it starts to curdle. The Suzette Butter can be prepared in advance and refrigerated or frozen until required.

When you are ready to serve, heat the Suzette Butter gently in a chafing dish or frying pan (this can be done on a side table in the dining room) and put the pancakes in one at a time, spooning the sauce over them. Fold each pancake in half and then in half again, push to the side of the pan and put in the next one.

When all the pancakes are folded and the sauce slightly reduced and thickened, pour over the orange liqueur. Warm the brandy in a ladle or small pan, tilt into the flame so that it ignites and pour over the pancakes. Shake the pan to liven the flames. Serve two pancakes for each helping and spoon on more sauce.

Prune and apricot snowballs

Metric

8 large prunes (soaked
overnight)
8 dried apricots (soaked
overnight)
40 g butter or margarine
150 ml water
75 g plain flour, sieved
2 eggs, beaten
Deep fat for frying
Crystallised ginger; or
glacé cherries; or
blanched almonds
50–75 g icing sugar, sieved

Imperial

8 large prunes (soaked
overnight)
8 dried apricots (soaked
overnight)
1½ oz butter or margarine
¼ pint water
3 oz plain flour, sieved
2 eggs, beaten
Deep fat for frying
Crystallised ginger; or
glacé cherries; or
blanched almonds
2–3 oz icing sugar, sieved

Little choux pastry fritters are filled with prunes or apricots stuffed with crystallised ginger, glacé cherries or blanched almonds. A wineglass of sherry added to the soaking water for the fruit improves the flavour.

Remove the prunes and apricots from the soaking liquid, slit down one side, remove prune stones and leave fruit to drain.

Dissolve the butter in the water over gentle heat, then bring to the boil and tip in the flour. Beat well with a wooden spoon over moderate heat until the dough forms a smooth ball. Add the beaten egg *very* gradually, beating well between each addition.

Stuff the drained fruit with a knob of ginger, a glacé cherry or a blanched almond and press firmly together. Heat fat to 190°C, 375°F. You can test it by dropping in a teaspoon of dough, which should rise at once to the surface and start to crisp. Take up tablespoons of the dough and drop them carefully into the hot fat. Use a teaspoon to push the dough off the tablespoon. Fry until puffed up, golden and crisp.

As each one is ready, remove from the fat with a slotted spoon, slit and stuff hollow centre with the stuffed fruit. Roll in the icing sugar and keep warm. Serve at once.

Greek almond fritters

Metric

50 g ground almonds
25 g caster sugar
¼ teaspoon ground
cinnamon
2–3 × 5 ml spoons lemon
juice
100 g plain shortcrust
Deep fat for frying
4 × 15 ml spoons honey
2 × 15 ml spoons orange
juice

Imperial

2 oz ground almonds
1 oz caster sugar
¼ teaspoon ground
cinnamon
2–3 teaspoons lemon
juice
4 oz plain shortcrust
Deep fat for frying
4 tablespoons honey
2 tablespoons orange
juice

Mix the almonds, sugar and cinnamon. Add the lemon juice and knead well together. Roll out the pastry very thinly and cut into 8 cm (3 in) squares. Put a small piece of filling in the centre of each square, damp the edges and fold over into triangles; press edges firmly together.

Heat the fat to 190°C, 375°F (a piece of dough dropped in should rise and crisp quickly). Fry the fritters a few at a time until golden all over. Drain on soft paper and keep warm while frying the next batch.

Heat the honey and orange juice together and dip in each fritter, coating it well. Serve hot as soon as possible. For parties you can make and fry the fritters in advance. Reheat them in a moderately hot oven and dip them into the orange honey syrup just before serving.

Vary the filling by using ground walnuts instead of almonds, or slit and seeded grapes.

Prune and apricot snowballs; Fluffy fruit fritters; Greek almond fritters

Fluffy fruit fritters

Metric

100 g plain flour
Pinch of salt
1 × 15 ml spoon corn oil
About 150 ml tepid water
2 egg whites
4 bananas, quartered; or 12
apple rings; or 12
pineapple rings
Deep fat for frying
Caster sugar for dredging
1 lemon

Imperial

4 oz plain flour
Pinch of salt
1 tablespoon corn oil
About ¼ pint tepid water
2 egg whites
4 bananas, quartered; or 12
apple rings; or 12
pineapple rings
Deep fat for frying
Caster sugar for dredging
1 lemon

Fruit fritters can be made with the basic pancake batter using 150 ml (¼ pint) milk to 100 g (4 oz) flour but this continental recipe gives a lighter, crisper result.

Sieve the flour and salt into a basin and make a well in the centre. Add the oil to the water and pour this liquid gradually into the well, stirring in the flour from the sides by degrees. When all the flour is incorporated add just sufficient liquid to make the batter coat the back of the wooden spoon. Beat well with a rotary whisk to ensure that the batter is free from lumps and well aerated. Allow to stand for 20 minutes or more for the flour to swell.

When ready to cook the fritters whisk the egg whites until stiff but not brittle and fold into the batter.

Heat the fat to 190°C, 375°F. (You can test it by dropping in a teaspoonful of batter, which will rise quickly and crisp if fat is the right temperature.) Using cooking tongs, dip pieces of fruit, one at a time, into batter, coat completely and draw over the rim of the bowl to allow surplus batter to run back. Lower carefully into hot fat. Do not try to fry too many fritters at once.

Watch the temperature of the fat between batches; if too low fritters will be greasy, if too hot they will burn. When a fritter is golden underneath, turn and fry other side. Remove from fat and drain on soft paper. Sprinkle with sugar and serve with lemon wedges.

Fruity griddle cakes

Metric

2 eggs, separated
125 g plain flour
2 × 5 ml spoons baking powder
2 × 15 ml spoons caster sugar
150 ml milk
1 × 15 ml spoon melted butter
2 apples or 2 bananas

To serve:
Warmed honey, golden syrup or lemon juice

Imperial

2 eggs, separated
4 oz plain flour
2 teaspoons baking powder
2 tablespoons caster sugar
¼ pint milk
1 tablespoon melted butter
2 apples or 2 bananas

To serve:
Warmed honey, golden syrup or lemon juice

For a quick and easy last-minute pudding Griddle Cakes are winners and handy for boating and sailing holidays. You can use a thick frying pan if you have no griddle. Whisk the egg whites until stiff. Sieve the flour, baking powder and 1 × 15 ml spoon (1 tablespoon) sugar into a bowl. Beat the egg yolks lightly and mix in with the milk and melted butter. Peel and coarsely grate the apples, discarding the core; or peel and chop bananas. Fold the fruit into the batter and then the whisked egg whites. Heat the griddle or frying pan and grease lightly. It is hot enough when a drop of water spits and splutters. Drop the batter on the hot griddle in tablespoons, allowing room for spreading. In a minute or two, when puffed and bubbly, flip over and brown the other side. Sprinkle with remaining sugar and serve with warmed honey, golden syrup or fresh lemon juice.

Cherry Clafoutis

Metric

450 g ripe cherries
2 eggs, beaten
50 g plain flour, sieved
50 g sugar
300 ml milk, warmed
1 tablespoon cherry brandy (optional)
25 g butter, melted
Caster sugar for dredging

Imperial

1 lb ripe cherries
2 eggs, beaten
2 oz plain flour, sieved
2 oz sugar
½ pint milk, warmed
1 tablespoon cherry brandy (optional)
1 oz butter, melted
Caster sugar for dredging

Cooking Time: 40 minutes
Oven 200°C, 400°F, Gas Mark 6;
        190°C, 375°F, Gas Mark 5

This is a French country dish from Limousin where they pour the batter over the juicy black cherries of the region. In winter use drained canned cherries.
Butter a shallow 600 ml (1 pint) ovenproof dish. A 20 cm (8 in) French pottery flan dish is ideal. Stalk and stone the cherries. Whisk eggs and gradually blend in flour and sugar. Slowly add warm milk, whisking steadily. Add cherry brandy if using and whisk in melted butter. Spread the prepared cherries over the base of the dish and pour the batter over them.
Bake in the centre of preheated oven for 20 minutes, then reduce heat slightly and continue cooking for 20 minutes or until the batter is well risen, golden and set. Serve hot, generously dredged with caster sugar.

Butterscotch upside down pudding

Metric

4 pineapple rings
4 cherries
100 g demerara sugar
50 g butter or margarine
50 g chopped walnuts

For the batter:
2 eggs, separated
¼ teaspoon vanilla essence
1 × 15 ml spoon melted butter
100 g caster sugar
100 g plain flour
1 × 5 ml spoon baking powder

Imperial

4 pineapple rings
4 cherries
4 oz demerara sugar
2 oz butter or margarine
2 oz chopped walnuts

For the batter:
2 eggs, separated
¼ teaspoon vanilla essence
1 tablespoon melted butter
4 oz caster sugar
4 oz plain flour
1 teaspoon baking powder

Cooking Time: 30 minutes
Oven: 160°C, 325°F, Gas Mark 3

Vary the fruit topping for this pudding by using apple rings, sliced pears or orange segments.
Grease a 20 cm (8 in) shallow cake tin and arrange the pineapple slices on the bottom with a cherry in the centre of each. Dissolve the sugar and melt the butter in a saucepan over gentle heat, then stir in the nuts. Mix well and pour over the pineapple slices.
Beat the egg yolks with the vanilla and melted butter until creamy. Whisk the egg whites until stiff but not brittle and fold in the sugar and the egg yolk mixture. Sieve together the flour and baking powder and fold in carefully. Pour the batter into the tin and spread it evenly. Bake in a preheated warm oven for 30 minutes or until firm and golden. Turn out upside down on a platter and serve hot or cold with cream.

Cherry Clafoutis; Fruity griddle cakes; Butterscotch upside down pudding

Plain shortcrust pastry

Metric	Imperial
225 g flour	8 oz flour
Pinch of salt	Pinch of salt
125 g fat	4 oz fat
Cold water to mix	Cold water to mix

Making pastry

Most pies and flans are made with a shortcrust pastry. Flaky and puff are for continental pastries. There are some golden rules for all pastries. Use cold ingredients, cold steel to mix and cold fingers to handle the dough. Sieve and aerate the flour. Rub in fat lightly with finger tips – don't squeeze it into marzipan. Add liquid carefully as too much makes heavy dough, too little makes it crumbly and difficult to roll out. Use short, firm rolls, lifting the pin frequently. Don't steam-roller out the air in the pastry or work in too much flour from the board. If sticky, chill before using.

This unsweetened pastry is quick and easy to make and does not need to be rested after mixing but can be used at once, either for baking or frying. Use either plain or self-raising flour, with butter, margarine, lard or vegetable shortening.

Sieve the flour and salt into a mixing bowl. Cut the fat into the flour and toss until well covered. Now rub it in with the tips of the fingers, lifting your hands well above the bowl to incorporate plenty of air.

When the mixture resembles breadcrumbs, shake the bowl and rub in any lumps which come to the surface. Add the cold water a little at a time, stirring with a rounded knife, until the mixture begins to bind. Now gather it up with your fingers and work it into a soft but not sticky dough, leaving the bowl clean. Do not over-knead it as it will become too elastic.

Spiced pear pie

Metric	Imperial
225 g plain shortcrust pastry (see above)	8 oz plain shortcrust pastry (see above)
40 g granulated sugar	1½ oz granulated sugar
40 g soft brown sugar	1½ oz soft brown sugar
1 × 15 ml spoon plain flour	1 tablespoon plain flour
¼ teaspoon grated nutmeg	¼ teaspoon grated nutmeg
¼ teaspoon ground cinnamon	¼ teaspoon ground cinnamon
Finely grated rind and juice of 1 orange	Finely grated rind and juice of 1 orange
Finely grated rind of ½ lemon	Finely grated rind of ½ lemon
1 × 15 ml spoon lemon juice	1 tablespoon lemon juice
900 g cooking pears	2 lb cooking pears
50 g sultanas	2 oz sultanas
40 g butter, melted	1½ oz butter, melted
To glaze:	To glaze:
Milk	Milk
Granulated sugar	Granulated sugar

Cooking Time: 45 minutes
Oven: 200°C, 400°F, Gas Mark 6;
      190°C, 375°F, Gas Mark 5

An exciting blend of flavours distinguish the filling of this double crust pie. The same recipe is excellent made with apples.

Light the oven and grease the base of a 20 cm (8 in) round shallow pie dish. Damp the lip of the dish.

Divide the pastry in half. Roll out one half thinly, line the pie dish and prick all over the base. Mix together the granulated sugar, brown sugar, flour and spices. Rub a little of the mixture over the pastry lining. Add the grated orange and lemon rind to the remainder.

Peel, core and slice the pears. Arrange them in layers in the dish, sprinkling each layer with sultanas, sugar mixture, fruit juices and melted butter.

Roll out the other piece of dough into a circle about 5 cm (2 in) larger all round than the top of the pie. Damp the edge of the lining pastry, lift the other piece on the rolling pin and unroll it across the top of the pie.

Press the two edges firmly together and with a sharp knife trim off the surplus dough. Knock the two edges together with the back of the knife and flute the edge. Make a few slits in the top of the pie to allow the steam from the fruit to escape. Brush lightly with milk and sprinkle with granulated sugar to give a glazed finish.

Bake in a moderately hot oven for 20 minutes until the pastry is well risen and turning colour; lower the heat and continue baking for 25 minutes or until the pie is cooked through. Serve hot with cream.

Treacle tart; Spiced pear pie

Treacle tart

Metric

175 g plain shortcrust
pastry (see opposite)
3 × 15 ml rounded spoons
golden syrup
1 × 5 ml spoon finely
grated lemon rind
2 × 15 ml rounded spoons
fresh white breadcrumbs

Imperial

6 oz plain shortcrust
pastry (see opposite)
3 rounded tablespoons
golden syrup
1 teaspoon finely grated
lemon rind
2 rounded tablespoons fresh
white breadcrumbs

Cooking Time: 30–35 minutes
Oven: 190°C, 375°F, Gas Mark 5

Grease the base, but not the lip, of a 20 cm (8 in) oven-proof plate or shallow pie dish. Roll the pastry out thinly into a circle. Cut strips off the outside edge the same width as the lip of the plate. Damp the lip and press on the pastry strip; damp the strip. Roll remaining pastry over the pin and unroll over the plate, ease it into the base of the plate and press outer edges firmly together. Trim off surplus pastry, knock-up outside edge with the back of a knife and flute it. Prick bottom of tart all over with a fork.

Warm the syrup with the lemon rind, mix in the breadcrumbs and pour into the tart. Cut pastry trimmings into narrow strips and criss-cross lattice fashion over the filling. Damp the ends of the strips and fix firmly on to pastry edge. Cover with little circles cut out of trimmings. Bake in the centre of preheated moderately hot oven for 30 minutes or until the pastry is crisp and golden. Serve hot or cold.

Sweet shortcrust pastry

Metric	Imperial
175 g plain flour	6 oz plain flour
Pinch of salt	Pinch of salt
50 g butter or margarine	2 oz butter or margarine
50 g lard or shortening	2 oz lard or shortening
2 × 5 ml spoons caster sugar	2 teaspoons caster sugar
1 egg yolk, beaten	1 egg yolk, beaten
Cold water to mix	Cold water to mix

This quantity is sufficient to line a flan case measuring 20–22 cm (8–9 in) across.

Sieve the flour and salt into a mixing bowl. Cut in the fat and toss until covered with flour. Rub in the fat with the tips of the fingers, lifting your hands well above the bowl to incorporate as much air as possible. Add the sugar and mix thoroughly.

Stir a tablespoon of water into the egg yolk and mix into the pastry. Stir in sufficient cold water, using a palette knife, to make a fairly stiff dough. Turn on to a floured board and knead lightly to remove cracks. Cover and put into a cool larder or refrigerator to relax for at least 30 minutes before rolling out.

Grapefruit meringue pie

Metric	Imperial
1 shortcrust flan case (18–20 cm) baked blind	1 shortcrust flan case (7–8 in) baked blind
2 × 15 ml spoons cornflour	2 tablespoons corn-flour
225 ml grapefruit juice	8 fl oz grapefruit juice
About 75 g caster sugar	About 3 oz caster sugar
2 egg yolks, beaten	2 egg yolks, beaten
For the meringue:	For the meringue:
2 egg whites	2 egg whites
50 g caster sugar, sieved	2 oz caster suger, sieved
Caster sugar for dredging	Caster sugar for dredging

Cooking Time: 30 minutes
Oven 160°C, 325°F, Gas Mark 3

This is a variation of the ever-popular Lemon Meringue Pie. You can use the small inexpensive fresh grapefruit or canned or frozen juice, which must be unsweetened to give the characteristic contrast of sharp filling and sweet topping. The flan case can be made with plain or sweet shortcrust.

Blend the cornflour with a little of the grapefruit juice to a smooth paste in a small saucepan. Gradually stir in remaining juice. Heat gradually, stirring continuously with a wooden spoon, then simmer gently for 3 minutes or until the mixture thickens and clears. Remove from heat and sweeten to taste. Cool slightly and gradually beat in the egg yolks. Pour into the flan case and smooth the top.

To make the meringue, whisk the egg whites until very stiff and dry. Fold in the sugar quickly and lightly. Spoon the meringue mixture round the outside edge of the pie and work towards the centre. Make sure the filling is completely covered and there are no little gaps round the pastry edge or the meringue will 'weep'. Dredge with caster sugar. Bake in the centre of a pre-heated moderate oven for 25–30 minutes or until set and golden coloured. Serve hot or cold, decorated with sugared grapefruit peel if available.

How to line a flan ring; How to bake blind; Grapefruit meringue pie

To line a flan ring

1. Place the ungreased flan ring on a greased baking tin. Roll out the pastry with quick jerky rolls into a circle about 6 mm ($\frac{1}{4}$ in) thick which will extend 4 cm ($1\frac{1}{2}$ in) beyond the flan ring all round.

2. Raise the pastry circle off the board and drop it gently back so that it can shrink before, and not during, cooking. Fold the pastry into a 5-sided shape small enough to fit inside the ring.

3. Lift it into the flan ring, open it out carefully easing (never stretching) it into the angle all round the base and press the pastry into the flutes with a floured finger.

4. Roll the rolling pin across the top of the flan ring to cut off the surplus pastry. Remove the trimmings.

To bake a flan case blind

1. Prick the base of the flan all over through to the tin. Line with a piece of greaseproof or buttered paper and cover with a layer of dried beans to keep the pastry flat during cooking.

2. Bake in a preheated moderately hot oven (200°C, 400°F, Gas Mark 6) for 15–20 minutes until the sides of the flan are set and crisp. Remove from the oven, lift out paper and beans (which you can use again) and return flan to oven for 5 minutes to crisp the base.

3. When removed from oven, allow the pastry to shrink slightly before lifting off the flan ring. Never lift flan up by the sides; slide a fish slice underneath.

Orange honey gingernut flan

Metric	Imperial
175 g ginger nuts	6 oz ginger nuts
50 g caster sugar	2 oz caster sugar
50 g butter, melted	2 oz butter, melted
For the filling:	**For the filling:**
225 g cottage cheese	8 oz cottage cheese
150 ml natural yogurt	$\frac{1}{4}$ pint natural yogurt
1 × 15 ml spoon orange blossom honey	1 tablespoon orange blossom honey
Finely grated rind and juice of 1 large orange	Finely grated rind and juice of 1 large orange
2 × 5 ml spoons powdered gelatine	2 teaspoons powdered gelatine
3 × 15 ml spoons hot water	3 tablespoons hot water
To decorate:	**To decorate:**
75 ml double cream	3 fl oz double cream
5 crystallised orange slices	5 crystallised orange slices

The crunchy case of this flan contrasts with the smooth sweet filling which is fresh and delicate in flavour, especially if you use a blossom-flavoured honey such as orange, heather or clover.

Crush the ginger nuts between 2 sheets of greaseproof paper with a rolling pin, or use a liquidiser. Combine with caster sugar and melted butter. Press into a 20 cm (8 in) pottery flan dish or shallow pie dish. Chill until firm in refrigerator.

Sieve the cottage cheese into a bowl and mix in yogurt and honey. Add the orange rind and juice. Dissolve the gelatine thoroughly in the hot water and stir into the mixture. Pour into the flan case and chill in refrigerator until set.

Decorate with piped whipped cream and crystallised orange slices cut into wedges.

Kentucky raisin pie

Metric	Imperial
175 g sweet shortcrust pastry (see page 50)	6 oz sweet shortcrust pastry (see page 50)
150 g seedless raisins	5 oz seedless raisins
$\frac{1}{4}$ teaspoon bicarbonate of soda	$\frac{1}{4}$ teaspoon bicarbonate of soda
4 × 15 ml spoons hot water	4 tablespoons hot water
50 g soft brown sugar	2 oz soft brown sugar
For the topping:	**For the topping:**
100 g plain flour	4 oz plain flour
$\frac{1}{2}$ teaspoon ground cinnamon	$\frac{1}{2}$ teaspoon ground cinnamon
$\frac{1}{4}$ teaspoon ground nutmeg	$\frac{1}{4}$ teaspoon ground nutmeg
$\frac{1}{4}$ teaspoon ground ginger	$\frac{1}{4}$ teaspoon ground ginger
50 g butter	2 oz butter
50 g soft brown sugar	2 oz soft brown sugar

Cooking Time: 30 minutes
Oven: 220°C, 425°F, Gas Mark 7;
   160°C, 325°F, Gas Mark 3

A sugar-and-spice pie which is a favourite with 'sweet tooths' of all ages.

Roll out the pastry thinly and line a 20 cm (8 in) greased pie plate. Pinch the edge of the pastry with finger and thumb into a decorative border. Prick the pastry base all over through to the plate and cover with raisins. Mix the bicarbonate of soda with the water and the brown sugar and pour it over the raisins.

Sieve the flour and spices together. Cut in the butter and rub it in with the tips of the fingers until the consistency of breadcrumbs. Mix in the sugar and spread over the raisin filling.

Bake in a preheated hot oven for 10 minutes until the pie begins to brown. Reduce the heat and continue cooking for 20 minutes until the filling is set. Serve hot or cold, with cream if wished.

Harlequin jam tart

Metric	Imperial
225 g plain shortcrust pastry (see page 48)	8 oz plain shortcrust pastry (see page 48)
1 × 15 ml spoon raspberry jam	1 tablespoon raspberry jam
1 × 15 ml spoon apricot jam	1 tablespoon apricot jam
1 × 15 ml spoon gooseberry jam	1 tablespoon gooseberry jam
1 × 15 ml spoon blackberry jam	1 tablespoon blackberry jam

Cooking Time: 30 minutes
Oven: 190°C, 375°F, Gas Mark 5

Roll the pastry out thinly and line a 20 cm (8 in) pie plate as for Treacle Tart (see page 49). With a knife mark the bottom pastry across into 8 equal triangles. Spread each triangle with jam, alternating the colours.
Cut the pastry trimmings into narrow strips and arrange them across the tart, dividing the jams. Damp the end of each strip, press one end on the pastry edge, twist it across the tart and secure on the other side. Cover the ends with cut out pastry shapes.
Bake in the centre of preheated moderately hot oven for 30 minutes.

Norfolk treacle custard tart

Metric	Imperial
125 g plain shortcrust pastry (see page 48)	4 oz plain shortcrust pastry (see page 48)
4 × 15 ml spoons golden syrup	4 tablespoons golden syrup
1 × 5 ml spoon finely grated lemon rind	1 teaspoon finely grated lemon rind
15 g butter	½ oz butter
2 × 15 ml spoons single cream	2 tablespoons single cream
1 egg, beaten	1 egg, beaten

Cooking Time: 40 minutes
Oven: 180°C, 350°F, Gas Mark 4

Roll pastry out thinly and line a 20 cm (8 in) flan ring (see page 51). Prick the bottom. Warm the syrup with the lemon rind. Cut the butter into small pieces and stir it into the syrup. Beat the cream and egg together and blend into the syrup. Pour into the flan case. Bake in the centre of a moderate oven for 40 minutes or until pastry is crisp and filling is set. Allow to shrink before removing flan ring and slide on to a serving plate. Serve hot or cold.

Orange honey gingernut flan; Kentucky raisin pie; Harlequin jam tart; Norfolk treacle custard tart

Cherry brandy pie

Metric

900 g cherries, stoned
75 g granulated sugar
225 g plain or sweet
shortcrust pastry (see page
48 or 50)
50 ml Cherry Brandy
75 ml double cream,
warmed
Caster sugar for dredging

Imperial

2 lb cherries, stoned
3 oz granulated sugar
8 oz plain or sweet
shortcrust pastry (see page
48 or 50)
2 fl oz Cherry Brandy
3 fl oz double cream,
warmed
Caster sugar for dredging

Cooking Time: 45 minutes
Oven: 200°C, 400°F, Gas Mark 6;
190°C, 375°F, Gas Mark 5

This is a party version of fruit pie, with cream and liqueur poured in under the lid. In Normandy they make it with apples and use Calvados (apple brandy).

Light the oven. Fill a 900 ml (1½ pint) oval pie dish with the stoned cherries, sugaring each layer.

Roll out the pastry thinly in an oval, 5 cm (2 in) wider than the top of the dish all round. Cut a strip of pastry, the same width as the lip of the dish, off the outside edge of the pastry. Damp the lip and press pastry strip firmly down on it. Damp the pastry strip, lift the rest of the pastry on the rolling pin and unroll it over the dish. Press the pastry edges together and trim off the surplus with a sharp knife. Holding the knife horizontally and using the back of it, knock up the pastry edge. Keep the thumb or crooked forefinger of the other hand on the pie, so the pastry is kept firmly pressed to the lip of the dish. Mark the outer edge neatly with the tines of a fork or flute it. Prick the top to allow the steam to escape.

Bake in the preheated moderately hot oven for 20 minutes, then reduce heat and continue cooking for 25 minutes until the fruit is cooked.

Remove from oven and cut neatly round the lid of the pie just inside the lip; lift off carefully. Pour the cherry brandy over the fruit and then the cream. Replace the lid, dredge with sugar and return to the oven for 5 minutes. Serve hot.

Coffee and walnut pie

Metric

175 g sweet shortcrust
pastry (see page 50)
2 × 15 ml spoons apricot
jam
75 g butter
75 g caster sugar
1 egg, beaten
40 g walnuts, finely
chopped
100 g self-raising flour
4 × 5 ml spoons liquid
coffee essence
1 × 15 ml spoon milk
150 ml soured cream

To decorate:
Walnuts, coarsely
chopped

Imperial

6 oz sweet shortcrust
pastry (see page 50)
2 tablespoons apricot
jam
3 oz butter
3 oz caster sugar
1 egg, beaten
1½ oz walnuts, finely
chopped
4 oz self-raising flour
4 teaspoons liquid coffee
essence
1 tablespoon milk
¼ pint soured cream

To decorate:
Walnuts, coarsely
chopped

Cooking Time: 45 minutes
Oven: 220°C, 425°F, Gas Mark 7;
160°C, 325°F, Gas Mark 3

Roll out pastry and line a 20 cm (8 in) flan ring. Prick base and spread with apricot jam. Cream butter and sugar together until light and fluffy; gradually beat in egg. Fold in walnuts and flour. Mix coffee essence with milk and blend into mixture. Turn into pastry case and smooth top.

Bake in the centre of preheated hot oven for 15 minutes. Reduce heat to moderate and bake for a further 25 minutes or until cooked; test with a skewer which should come out clean. Warm soured cream, but do not overheat. Pour over pie and return to oven for 5 minutes. Remove from the oven, scatter chopped walnuts on top and serve immediately.

This pie is also very good served cold: spread lemon-flavoured glacé icing over the filling instead of the soured cream and decorate with walnut halves.

Winter fruit salad

Metric	Imperial
For the salad:	For the salad:
50 g dried apricots	*2 oz dried apricots*
50 g prunes or dried pears	*2 oz prunes or dried pears*
50 g dried peaches	*2 oz dried peaches*
50 g dried apple rings	*2 oz dried apple rings*
100 g green grapes, seeded	*4 oz green grapes, seeded*
For the syrup:	For the syrup:
600 ml dried fruit liquor	*1 pint dried fruit liquor*
175 g granulated sugar	*6 oz granulated sugar*
1 thin sliver lemon rind	*1 thin sliver lemon rind*

Dried fruit, nicely prepared, makes an excellent compote or salad. You can also mix in fresh fruit available in winter, such as orange sections or green grapes.

Put the dried fruit in a large bowl, cover with 1·2 l (2 pints) of water and soak overnight.

Measure off 600 ml (1 pint) of the liquor, add the sugar and lemon rind and make syrup as below. Drain fruit, add to prepared syrup and simmer gently for 20 minutes. Mix in seeded green grapes.

Serve hot or well-chilled with Lemon Flummery, cream or custard.

To make syrup for fruit salad
According to the sweetness required, use 175–350 g (6–12 oz) of sugar to 600 ml (1 pint) of water or dried fruit liquor. Add a thin sliver of lemon or orange rind, a vanilla pod, a stick of cinnamon or a blade of mace for flavour. Boil briskly for about 5 minutes, reduce heat and add the fruit, which should be just covered. You can also flavour with rum, sherry or liqueur.

Lemon flummery

Metric	Imperial
300 ml water	*½ pint water*
25 g butter	*1 oz butter*
Finely grated rind and juice of 1 lemon	*Finely grated rind and juice of 1 lemon*
25 g plain flour	*1 oz plain flour*
100 g caster sugar	*4 oz caster sugar*
1 egg, separated	*1 egg, separated*

Heat the water with the butter and lemon rind. Mix the flour and sugar in a bowl. Gradually stir in the hot liquid, beating smooth. Blend a little of this mixture into the beaten egg yolk. Mix this back into the mixture and pour all back into the saucepan. Cook gently for 5 minutes. Add the lemon juice and pour into a cold bowl. Whisk the egg white until stiff but not dry and fold into the flummery. Serve hot or cold with baked fruit, fruit compotes etc.

Fluffy fruit fool

Metric	Imperial
150 ml milk	*¼ pint milk*
2 eggs, separated	*2 eggs, separated*
300 ml sweetened rhubarb purée (see opposite)	*½ pint sweetened rhubarb purée (see opposite)*
150 ml double cream	*¼ pint double cream*
Sugar to taste	*Sugar to taste*

Fruit fools are easily made. Usually they consist of fruit purée blended with cornflour or egg custard and/or whipped cream. In this recipe the whisked egg whites are also folded into the fool which gives it a lighter texture and makes it suitable for freezing.

Warm the milk and add gradually to the beaten egg yolks. Pour back into the rinsed saucepan. Stir over gentle heat until the mixture thickens and clings to the back of the wooden spoon. Chill thoroughly and mix into the rhubarb purée. Whip the cream fairly stiff and fold in. Sweeten to taste. Whisk the egg whites until stiff but not brittle and fold into the fool. Pour into goblets and chill until required. Serve topped with baby meringues or ratafias; accompany with biscuits or sponge fingers.

Lemon flummery; Winter fruit salad; Fluffy fruit fool

Fruit purée

Fruit purée is an important ingredient in many desserts. If it is thin and watery it will spoil the dish; it must be thick and full of flavour. The fruit can be cooked in a saucepan on top of the stove, or in a casserole in a moderate oven (180°C, 350°F, Gas Mark 4). Do not add sugar until the fruit is cooked as it will toughen the skins. 450 g (1 lb) of fresh fruit yields about 300 ml ($\frac{1}{2}$ pint) of purée.

Apricots, plums
Wash under running cold water. Cut round the fruit in the natural crease down to the stone. Twist the two halves in opposite directions so that the fruit splits and the stones can be removed. Cover the base of a thick saucepan with water. Add the fruit and cook gently until juice runs. Remove lid and continue cooking until liquid has evaporated. Sieve fruit or mash in a blender. Sweeten to taste.

Raspberries, loganberries, strawberries
These do not need to be cooked to make a purée, but must be sieved if you want to get rid of the pips.

Apples
Quarter, peel thinly, remove cores and slice into a bowl of cold water with 2 × 15 ml spoons (2 tablespoons) of lemon juice to prevent discoloration. Butter the bottom of a thick saucepan. Put in the drained apples and 2 × 15 ml spoons (2 tablespoons) water. Cover and cook gently until juice begins to flow. Remove lid and continue cooking until apples are soft and liquid has evaporated, stirring gently from time to time. Beat into a smooth thick purée with a wooden spoon. Add sugar to taste.

Gooseberries, blackberries, redcurrants
Top and tail the fruit with scissors. Wash under running cold water and cook as apricots.

Rhubarb
Cut off the leaves (which contain unwholesome oxalic acid), and the thick white ends of the stalks. Wash or wipe the stalks clean and chop into 2·5 cm (1 in) lengths. Put into a buttered pan with a sliver of orange rind or two tablespoons orange juice and cook as apples.

Berries with cointreau chantilly

Metric	Imperial
350 g strawberries	12 oz strawberries
175 ml whipping cream	6 fl oz whipping cream
175 ml single cream	6 fl oz single cream
2 × 15 ml spoons caster sugar	2 tablespoons caster sugar
1–2 × 15 ml spoons Cointreau	1–2 tablespoons Cointreau
To decorate:	To decorate:
Crushed meringues or ratafias	Crushed meringues or ratafias
Crystallised mint leaves	Crystallised mint leaves

Hull the strawberries. Whip the two creams together until stiff and fold in the sugar. Flavour to taste with Cointreau. Fold in the prepared berries and spoon into individual glasses. Chill until required.

Serve topped with crushed meringues or ratafias and garnished with crystallised mint leaves.

Strawberries, raspberries, loganberries or cultivated blackberries can all be used in this quickly-prepared and delicious sweet. Flavour with Cointreau, Grand Marnier, Orange Curaçao or Kirsch according to taste and availability.

Honeydew and pineapple basket

Metric	Imperial
1 ripe honeydew melon	1 ripe honeydew melon
4 slices pineapple, fresh or canned	4 slices pineapple, fresh or canned
3–4 × 15 ml spoons condensed milk (sweet)	3–4 tablespoons condensed milk (sweet)
50 g ground almonds	2 oz ground almonds
1 × 15 ml spoon lemon juice	1 tablespoon lemon juice

Cut top third off melon and discard pips. Scoop flesh out of both parts with a sharp spoon and cut in pieces. Vandyke the edges of melon shells by cutting small triangles all around to give a zig-zag effect.

Chop the pineapple and mix with melon flesh, condensed milk, ground almonds and lemon juice. Pack this mixture into larger melon shell and pile it up in the centre. Put melon lid on at an angle and secure at back with cocktail sticks. Wrap melon completely in clingfilm or foil and chill thoroughly. Serve garnished with fresh leaves and/or flowers and crushed ice.

French apple and ginger cake

Metric	Imperial
225 g caster sugar	8 oz caster sugar
150 ml cider	¼ pint cider
150 ml water	¼ pint water
2 × 15 ml spoons ginger syrup	2 tablespoons ginger syrup
Piece of thin lemon rind	Piece of thin lemon rind
900 g dessert apples	2 lb dessert apples
50 g sultanas	2 oz sultanas
50 g chopped preserved ginger	2 oz chopped preserved ginger
To decorate:	To decorate:
150 ml double cream	¼ pint double cream
Preserved ginger	Preserved ginger

This dessert should be made well in advance so that it can be thoroughly chilled, preferably overnight. It is also very good made with pears. Use ginger preserved in syrup, not the sugary crystallised ginger.

Line the base of an 18–20 cm (7–8 in) cake tin with kitchen foil and brush all over lightly with oil.

Dissolve the sugar in the cider and water, add the ginger syrup and lemon rind and bring to the boil. Wash and core the apples, slice thinly and add to the syrup. Simmer very gently, without a lid, until the apple slices are transparent. Stir occasionally, taking care not to break the slices.

When the apple slices are cooked, lift them out of the syrup with a draining spoon and arrange in layers in the tin, sprinkling each layer with sultanas and chopped ginger. When all the apple is in cover with a heavy oiled plate which fits in the top of the tin. Chill in the refrigerator, preferably overnight.

To serve remove plate and place a large platter over the tin. Invert both together quickly, and carefully remove the tin and foil. Decorate the cake with piped whipped cream and preserved ginger.

Berries with cointreau chantilly; French apple and ginger cake; Honeydew and pineapple basket

Apricot amber; Flamed Jamaican bananas

Apricot amber

Metric	Imperial
300 ml sweetened apricot purée, still warm	½ pint sweetened apricot purée, still warm
Lemon juice to taste	Lemon juice to taste
25 g butter	1 oz butter
2 eggs, separated	2 eggs, separated
50 g caster sugar	2 oz caster sugar

Cooking Time: 30–35 minutes
Oven: 160°C, 325°F, Gas Mark 3

Sharpen the purée to taste with lemon juice. Stir in the butter and beaten egg yolks. Pour the mixture into a greased shallow pie dish. Whisk the egg whites to a stiff snow and fold in the caster sugar. Cover the fruit mixture completely with the meringue and ruffle the top. Dredge with caster sugar. Bake in the centre of a warm oven for 30 minutes or until meringue is crisp and golden. Serve hot or cold.

You can make this pudding equally well with any fruit purée. For a more hearty dish bake in a shortcrust pastry case.

Flamed Jamaican bananas

Metric	Imperial
4 large under-ripe bananas	4 large under-ripe bananas
40 g butter	1½ oz butter
Juice of ½ large lemon	Juice of ½ large lemon
2 × 15 ml spoons rum	2 tablespoons rum
To serve:	To serve:
Brown sugar	Brown sugar
Single cream	Single cream

Peel the bananas and halve lengthwise. Heat the butter in a flameproof dish and fry the bananas, cut side down. When golden, turn over, sprinkle with lemon juice, and fry until the underneath is colouring. Warm the rum in a ladle, ignite and pour over bananas. Serve while still flaming with a bowl of brown sugar and a jug of cream. If no flameproof dish is available use a frying pan.

Fresh pineapple pyramid

Fresh pineapple pyramid

Metric

1 medium pineapple
3–4 × 15 ml spoons caster sugar
175 ml double cream
2 × 15 ml spoons Kirsch (optional)
225 g strawberries; or raspberries; or cherries

Imperial

1 medium pineapple
3–4 tablespoons caster sugar
6 fl oz double cream
2 tablespoons Kirsch (optional)
8 oz strawberries; or raspberries; or cherries

This fresh fruit dessert makes an attractive dish on buffet or dinner tables. Be sure to choose a pineapple with a top of fresh green leaves. In winter orange or mandarin sections can replace the summer fruit.

Cut the top off the pineapple complete with leaves and set aside. Level off the bottom and discard the fibrous base. Stand the pineapple on a chopping board and with a large sharp knife, working downwards from the top, cut off the skin all round. Cut the pineapple across in thick slices – 1·5 cm ($\frac{1}{2}$ in). Remove the core from each slice with an apple corer and sprinkle with sugar. Whip the cream stiffly, sweeten to taste and add Kirsch if using. Hull and halve the strawberries, pick over the raspberries or stone the cherries.

Reform the pineapple in an upright position on a serving platter, spreading a layer of cream covered with prepared fruit between each slice. Replace the top, with leaves, wrap in clingfilm and refrigerate until required. When serving use a pastry slice to remove top and serve one slice complete with whipped cream and strawberries to each guest.

61

Hot chocolate soufflé

Metric	Imperial
100 g plain chocolate	4 oz plain chocolate
4 × 15 ml spoons black coffee	4 tablespoons black coffee
40 g butter	1½ oz butter
40 g plain flour	1½ oz plain flour
225 ml milk	8 fl oz milk
50 g caster sugar	2 oz caster sugar
¼ teaspoon vanilla essence	¼ teaspoon vanilla essence
3 egg yolks	3 egg yolks
4 egg whites	4 egg whites
Icing sugar to glaze	Icing sugar to glaze

To serve:

150 ml single cream	¼ pint single cream
2–3 × 15 ml spoons rum or Tia Maria	2–3 tablespoons rum or Tia Maria

Cooking Time: 25–30 minutes
Oven: 190°C, 375°F, Gas Mark 5

Chocolate is a rich, rather heavy ingredient and it is essential to use an extra egg white in this soufflé to get a really light, fluffy texture.

Prepare a 15 cm (6 in) soufflé dish and the oven (see page 62). Break up chocolate and put in a bowl with the black coffee over a saucepan of hot water to melt.

Melt butter in a small saucepan, remove from heat and blend in flour. Gradually add milk, bring to the boil and simmer, stirring, for 3 minutes. Stir melted chocolate until smooth and blend into the sauce. Stir in sugar until dissolved and the vanilla. Remove from heat, cool slightly and gradually beat in egg yolks.

Whisk the egg whites until stiff but not brittle, in a large bowl. Pour over the chocolate mixture, about a third at a time, and fold it in quickly and lightly.

Pour into prepared soufflé dish. With a teaspoon dig a little trench, about 1·5 cm (½ in) deep, about 2·5 cm (1 in) from the rim of the dish all round. This will give a 'crown' to the soufflé when it rises.

When the soufflé has baked for 25 minutes, draw the oven shelf forward, dredge with icing sugar and return to the oven for 5 minutes to caramelise. Serve immediately with cream flavoured with rum or Tia Maria. The liqueur can be added to the soufflé mixture, but as it is very volatile in hot mixtures it will have more effect in the cream.

To prepare a soufflé dish
Choose the right size so the soufflé can rise well above the dish. For a 2-egg soufflé, use a 13 cm (5 in) dish; for a 3-egg soufflé a 15 cm (6 in) dish and for a 4-egg soufflé an 18 cm (7 in) dish. Cut a band of double greaseproof paper long enough to overlap by 5 cm (2 in) round the dish and wide enough to stand 8 cm (3 in) above it. Grease the inside of the dish and the top half of the paper band. Wrap it round the outside of the dish with the fold at the base and secure with string.

To prepare the oven for a soufflé
Move top shelf to centre of oven and preheat to required temperature (190°C, 375°F, Gas Mark 5). If the temperature is too low the soufflé texture will be dry like sponge cake. It should be well risen, the top golden and firm to the touch but the centre still soft and creamy.

Points to watch
1. The basis of a hot soufflé is a butter and flour roux made into a thick sauce with milk, coffee, fruit juice or purée, into which the egg yolks are beaten. Cool slightly before adding yolks or they will curdle.
2. Do not try to fold the whisked egg whites into the sauce in a small saucepan. Pour the sauce over the whisked egg whites in a large bowl, about a third at a time; fold and cut it in lightly and quickly.
3. Do not remove paper collar until serving as a cold draught can collapse the soufflé in minutes.

Hot chocolate soufflé

Steamed apricot soufflé

Metric
300 ml apricot purée
40 g butter
40 g plain flour
Sugar to taste
3 egg yolks, beaten
1 × 15 ml spoon lemon juice
3–4 egg whites
2 × 15 ml spoons flaked almonds
Apricot sauce (see page 28)

Imperial
½ pint apricot purée
1½ oz butter
1½ oz plain flour
Sugar to taste
3 egg yolks, beaten
1 tablespoon lemon juice
3–4 egg whites
2 tablespoons flaked almonds
Apricot sauce (see page 28)

Cooking Time: 1 hour
Oven: 190°C, 375°F, Gas Mark 5

Stewed fresh, dried or canned fruit can be used for this recipe. Strain and purée the fruit, measure and make up to 300 ml (½ pint) with the liquid. Use the surplus liquid for the sauce. The amount of sugar to use in the soufflé mixture will depend on the original sweetness of the purée. Greengages, plums, raspberries, loganberries or blackberries can replace the apricots.

Prepare a 15 cm (6 in) soufflé dish and the oven (see page 62). Melt butter in a small saucepan, remove from heat and blend in flour. Stir in the apricot purée, bring to the simmer and cook, stirring for 3–5 minutes. Sweeten to taste. Cool slightly and gradually beat in egg yolks. Add lemon juice. Whisk egg whites into a stiff but not dry snow and fold into mixture. Pour into prepared soufflé dish and stand it in a roasting tin with sufficient cold water to come halfway up. Bake for 1 hour, or until set and springy to the touch.

Meanwhile toast flaked almonds under the grill and make the sauce. When the soufflé is ready, brush the top with a little of the sauce and sprinkle on the almonds. Serve immediately, with the sauce separately.

Cold sweet soufflés

Cold soufflé is made quite differently from hot soufflé, with a custard base into which whipped cream and whisked egg whites are folded. It is not baked, but set with gelatine. The setting mixture is poured into a soufflé dish with a paper collar like a hot soufflé (see page 62) so that it stands 7 cm (3 in) above the top of the dish. It makes an impressive and delicious cold dessert for parties with no risk of collapse.

Points to watch

1. Take care to dissolve the gelatine completely before adding it to the basic mixture as it will not melt later but leave little nodules in the finished soufflé, which also may not set owing to insufficient melted gelatine.
2. Do not over-whip the egg whites. They must be stiff, but if they are too dry and brittle it will be difficult to fold them in smoothly.
3. Do not be tempted to fold the whisked egg whites into the setting mixture until it is thick and heavy, or it will separate as it sets into a jelly in the base of the dish with foam on top. If the mixture is slightly too set, whisk again before folding in the cream and egg whites.

Steamed apricot soufflé; Preparing a soufflé dish

Fresh orange and lemon soufflé

Metric	Imperial
3 eggs, separated	3 eggs, separated
175 g caster sugar	6 oz caster sugar
100 ml orange juice	4 fl oz orange juice
50 ml lemon juice	2 fl oz lemon juice
12 g (1 envelope) powdered gelatin	½ oz (1 envelope) powdered gelatine
300 ml whipping cream; or	½ pint whipping cream; or
150 ml evaporated milk, with 1 × 15 ml spoon lemon juice	¼ pint evaporated milk, with 1 tablespoon lemon juice
2 × 15 ml spoons Orange Curaçao, Cointreau or Grand Marnier (optional)	2 tablespoons Orange Curaçao, Cointreau or Grand Marnier (optional)

To decorate:
Crystallised orange and lemon slices
Pistachio nuts or angelica
Double cream (optional)

To decorate:
Crystallised orange and lemon slices
Pistachio nuts or angelica
Double cream (optional)

This is a light, refreshing dessert to follow a rich main course. The proportion of orange to lemon juice can be varied to taste. Orange juice by itself tends to be insipid and needs sharpening with lemon or grapefruit.

Prepare a 15 cm (6 in) soufflé dish (see page 62). Whisk the egg yolks, sugar and fruit juice in a large bowl over a saucepan of boiling water (take care the water does not touch the bowl), until the mixture is thick and foamy and falls from the whisk in ribbons which hold their shape for a few seconds before sinking back into the mixture. Remove from heat. Dissolve the gelatine in a cup with 3–4 × 15 ml spoons (3–4 tablespoons) of the boiling water from the pan. When thoroughly dissolved, whisk into the fruit mixture. Set aside to chill and thicken. Whisk the egg whites until stiff but not brittle. Whip the cream to a soft peak. (If using evaporated milk, whisk it with a tablespoon of lemon juice until it doubles in bulk.) When the fruit mixture has thickened and is beginning to set, fold in the cream and then the egg whites. Fold in the liqueur last. Turn the mixture into the soufflé dish, smooth the top and refrigerate until set. Peel off the paper collar with the help of a knife dipped in hot water. Cut the orange and lemon slices into small wedges, halve or chop the pistachio nuts (or angelica) and decorate to taste, with whipped cream if using. Stand the soufflé dish on a dessert plate to serve.

Coffee praline soufflé

Metric	Imperial
For the praline:	For the praline:
50 g caster sugar	2 oz caster sugar
50 g unblanched almonds	2 oz unblanched almonds
For the soufflé:	For the soufflé:
3 eggs, separated	3 eggs, separated
75 g caster sugar	3 oz caster sugar
2 × 15 ml spoons instant coffee granules	2 tablespoons instant coffee granules
175 ml boiling water	6 fl oz boiling water
12 g (1 envelope) powdered gelatine	½ oz (1 envelope) powdered gelatine
3 × 15 ml spoons cold water	3 tablespoons cold water
300 ml double cream	½ pint double cream
2 × 15 ml spoons Tia Maria (optional)	2 tablespoons Tia Maria (optional)

Prepare a 15 cm (6 in) soufflé dish. First make the praline so that it has time to cool. Put the sugar and almonds into a small thick saucepan over gentle heat. When the sugar is dissolved, stir carefully to coat the almonds and continue cooking until rich golden brown and smelling of toffee. Pour on to an oiled baking tin, spreading it out. When cold and brittle, remove and chop small or grind in a mill, but not to fine powder.

Mix the egg yolks and sugar in a large bowl. Dissolve the coffee in the boiling water and add gradually. Whisk over a saucepan of boiling water until thick and foamy. Remove from heat and continue whisking until cold. Soak the gelatine in the cold water, dissolve over gentle heat and stir into the soufflé mixture. Place in a basin of cold water with ice and stir gently from time to time until beginning to set.

Meanwhile whisk egg whites until stiff but not dry. Whip cream into soft peaks and fold about two-thirds into the coffee mixture. Fold in egg whites and half the praline. Mix in the Tia Maria if using. Turn into the soufflé dish, smooth top and chill. When set, peel off paper collar with the help of a knife dipped in hot water. Coat the sides of the soufflé with some of the remaining praline. Whip remaining cream stiff enough to pipe and decorate the top of the soufflé. Garnish with the rest of the praline.

Coffee praline soufflé; Fresh orange and lemon soufflé

Variations

Raspberry, loganberry or apricot soufflé
Follow the recipe for Orange and Lemon Soufflé and use a purée of fresh, frozen or canned fruit instead of the juice. If using canned fruit, strain off the juice, then purée the fruit, measure and make up to 175 ml (6 fl oz) with juice. This gives you a good thick purée.
Sharpen the soufflé mixture with lemon juice to taste just before folding in the egg whites. If adding liqueurs Kirsch is a good choice with Raspberry and Loganberry Soufflé; apricot brandy with the Apricot.

Fresh Tangerine soufflé
Follow the recipe for Orange and Lemon Soufflé, using tangerine instead of orange juice. Kirsch or the orange based liqueurs are suitable for flavouring. Decorate with tangerine segments, or the rind blanched in boiling water and cut into an attractive design.

Fresh grapefruit soufflé
Follow the recipe for Orange and Lemon Soufflé using 100 ml (4 fl oz) grapefruit juice and 50 ml (2 fl oz) orange juice instead of lemon.

67

Honey and lemon milk jelly

Metric	Imperial
2 large eggs, separated	2 large eggs, separated
2 × 15 ml spoons honey, warmed	2 tablespoons honey, warmed
Finely grated rind and juice of 1 lemon	Finely grated rind and juice of 1 lemon
600 ml creamy milk	1 pint creamy milk
12 g (1 envelope) powdered gelatine	½ oz (1 envelope) powdered gelatine
2 × 15 ml spoons hot water	2 tablespoons hot water

Beat the egg yolks and honey together until creamy. Add lemon rind to the milk and heat slowly in a thick saucepan without boiling. Whisk a little hot milk into the egg yolk mixture and blend this into the hot milk. Stir over gentle heat until the custard clings to the back of the wooden spoon. Strain into a cold bowl and cool. Dissolve gelatine thoroughly in the hot water and stir into the custard with the lemon juice. Whisk the egg whites until stiff but not brittle and fold into the custard. Reheat until nearly boiling. Rinse a 900 ml (1½ pint) jelly mould with cold water, pour in mixture slowly, cool and then refrigerate until set. It will separate as it sets into a fluffy top and lemon jelly base which will be reversed when it is unmoulded. Serve with fruit compote or fresh summer fruit, and cream.

Fresh apricot jelly

Metric	Imperial
225 g granulated sugar	8 oz granulated sugar
600 ml water	1 pint water
1 thin piece lemon peel	1 thin piece lemon peel
450 g fresh apricots	1 lb fresh apricots
12 g (1 envelope) powdered gelatine	½ oz (1 envelope) powdered gelatine
3 × 15 ml spoons hot water	3 tablespoons hot water
To serve:	To serve:
Crumbled meringues or ratafias	Crumbled meringues or ratafias
Whipping cream or single cream	Whipping cream or single cream

A fruit jelly is an agreeable way to use apricots, greengages, plums, or peaches which are slightly underripe. Dissolve the sugar in the water. Add the lemon rind and boil for 5 minutes. Add the apricots and cook gently for 10–15 minutes; do not overcook. Lift the fruit out with a draining spoon on to a plate. Remove skins, put these back in the simmering syrup and continue cooking to reduce slightly.
Meanwhile halve and stone the apricots and put them in a glass serving bowl, or divide between individual dishes. Strain and measure off 600 ml (1 pint) of apricot syrup. Dissolve the gelatine in the hot water and stir into the syrup. Pour over the fruit and leave in a cool place to set. Serve decorated with whipped cream and crumbled meringues or accompany with a jug of pouring cream.

Fruit Chartreuse

Metric	Imperial
135 g packet lemon jelly	4¾ oz packet lemon jelly
312 g can mandarins	11 oz can mandarins
225 g cherries or grapes	8 oz cherries or grapes
4 ripe bananas	4 ripe bananas
Juice of 1 lemon	Juice of 1 lemon
To decorate:	To decorate:
Whipping cream	Whipping cream

This colourful dessert is not so difficult to make as it looks. The secret is patience – set one layer at a time or the fruit will swim about and lose its pattern. Choose any fruits of contrasting colour.
Break up the jelly and dissolve in 300 ml (½ pint) boiling water. Add the drained mandarin juice and sufficient cold water to make liquid up to 600 ml (1 pint). Stone cherries or seed grapes. Peel bananas and cut each across into 3 equal pieces. Brush with lemon juice to prevent discoloration.
Rinse out a shallow 900 ml (1½ pint) jelly mould with cold water. Pour a thin layer of jelly over the base and refrigerate until set. When firm arrange mandarin sections and cherries or grapes in an attractive pattern on it, dipping each piece in liquid jelly first. Chill until firm, then cover with a layer of jelly and chill. When set, stand banana sticks round sides of mould, dipping each piece in liquid jelly. Fill centre with mixed fruit, cover with more jelly to fill mould and refrigerate. To serve, unmould and decorate with piped whipped cream and any remaining fruit.

Fresh apricot jelly; Fruit chartreuse; Honey and lemon milk jelly

Chocolate cream ice

Metric	Imperial
50 g plain chocolate	2 oz plain chocolate
600 ml single cream	1 pint single cream
75 g caster sugar	3 oz caster sugar
3 egg yolks, beaten	3 egg yolks, beaten
2–3 × 15 ml spoons	2–3 tablespoons Marsala
Marsala or sweet sherry	or sweet sherry

To decorate:	To decorate:
Whipping cream	Whipping cream
Crystallised violets	Crystallised violets
Pistacho nuts or walnuts	Pistachio nuts or walnuts

An ice-cream made with a chocolate custard base which can be varied by flavouring it with instant coffee or rum, or given a crunchy texture by folding in 2–3 × 15 ml spoons (2–3 tablespoons) of praline (see page 66) with the egg whites.

Break up chocolate and melt in a bowl over hot water. Put the cream over gentle heat. Add a little hot cream to the melted chocolate, stir until smooth and blend back into cream with the sugar. Add 2–3 × 15 ml spoons (2–3 tablespoons) of the chocolate mixture to the egg yolks and stir this mixture back into the pan. Continue to stir over gentle heat (in a double boiler if preferred) until cream thickens into a thin custard and coats the back of the wooden spoon. Do not boil or it will separate.

Cool, stirring occasionally to prevent a skin forming, then add Marsala or sherry. Pour into freezing tray or moulds and freeze until stiff. Serve decorated with whipped cream, crystallised violets and chopped nuts.

Slimline orange sorbet

Metric	Imperial
175 ml frozen or fresh orange juice	6 fl oz frozen or fresh orange juice
1 large orange	1 large orange
300 ml natural yogurt	½ pint natural yogurt
12 g (1 envelope) powdered gelatine	½ oz (1 envelope) powdered gelatine
4 × 15 ml spoons hot water	4 tablespoons hot water
2 egg whites	2 egg whites
To garnish:	To garnish:
Fresh mint or borage sprigs	Fresh mint or borage sprigs

A refreshing water ice made without sugar, this will have special appeal for calorie-counting guests.

Defrost the frozen orange juice. Grate the rind finely off the orange and add to the juice. Mix into the yogurt. Dissolve the gelatine in hot water, blend with the mixture and leave to thicken.

Whisk the egg whites to a stiff snow and when the yogurt begins to set, fold in carefully. Pour the sorbet mixture into a freezer container and freeze.

Peel the pith off the orange. Take a sharp knife and cut down to the centre of the orange on either side of each section and lift it out from between the dividing membranes.

To serve fill individual glasses with spoonfuls of frozen sorbet interspersed with orange sections. Garnish with sprigs of fresh mint or borage.

Brown bread ice-cream

Metric	Imperial
175 ml double cream crumbs	3 oz wholemeal bread-crumbs
100 g caster sugar	4 oz caster sugar
175 ml double cream	6 fl oz double cream
100 ml single cream	4 fl oz single cream
100 g icing sugar, sieved	4 oz icing sugar, sieved
1 egg, separated	1 egg, separated
2 × 15 ml spoons rum or Marsala	2 tablespoons rum or Marsala

To decorate:	To decorate:
50 g crushed peanut brittle or praline (see page 66)	2 oz crushed peanut brittle or praline (see page 66)
Whipping cream (optional	Whipping cream (optional)

A modern version of the popular Victorian ice-cream which may sound a little dull but tastes delicious.

Spread the crumbs on a baking tray and sprinkle with the caster sugar. Bake in a moderately hot oven until crisp and golden, shaking the tray from time to time. Spread on a cold plate to cool.

Whisk the double and single cream together, gradually adding the icing sugar. Beat the egg yolk with the rum or Marsala and whisk into the cream.

Whisk the egg white until stiff but not brittle and fold into the mixture with the breadcrumbs. Turn into a 600 ml (1 pint) mould, cover tightly with foil and freeze. To unmould dip briskly into hot water and turn out. Decorate with crushed peanut brittle or praline and serve with butterscotch or chocolate sauce. Alternatively serve in individual glasses, pour over the sauce, top with whipped cream and nut brittle.

Brown bread ice-cream; Chocolate cream ice; Iced plum pudding; Slimline orange sorbet

Iced plum pudding

Metric

300 ml double cream
225 g can condensed milk
1 × 5 ml spoon mixed
spice
½ teaspoon grated nutmeg
4 × 5 ml spoons instant
coffee powder
25 g chopped citron peel
50 g chopped walnuts
75 g seedless raisins
75 g sultanas
75 g glacé cherries,
chopped
Finely grated rind of 1
orange
½ teaspoon vanilla essence
2–3 × 15 ml spoons rum or
brown sherry

To decorate:
1 tangerine
1–2 × 15 ml spoons rum or
brandy

Imperial

½ pint double cream
8 oz can condensed milk
1 teaspoon mixed
spice
½ teaspoon grated nutmeg
4 teaspoons instant coffee
powder
1 oz chopped citron peel
2 oz chopped walnuts
3 oz seedless raisins
3 oz sultanas
3 oz glacé cherries,
chopped
Finely grated rind of 1
orange
½ teaspoon vanilla essence
2–3 tablespoons rum or
brown sherry

To decorate:
1 tangerine
1–2 tablespoons rum or
brandy

This is a recipe from Australia where Christmas falls in the hottest days of summer and hot Christmas pudding may not be too welcome.

Whisk half of the cream together with the condensed milk, spices and coffee. Pour into a refrigerator tray and freeze until stiffened. Turn into a bowl and whisk again until light and creamy. Whip remaining cream to soft peak and fold into the mixture with the fruit, nuts and orange rind. Flavour to taste with vanilla and rum or sherry. Pour into a pudding mould and freeze hard.

Move mould from freezer to refrigerator about 1 hour before required. Cut tangerine in half; carefully scoop out pulp from one half.

To serve, dip mould quickly into hot water and unmould on to a serving platter. Make a hollow in the top and place a half tangerine shell inside. Warm 1 or 2 table-spoons rum, fill the shell, set alight and serve immediately.

Iced raspberry parfait

Metric	Imperial
450 g fresh raspberries	1 lb fresh raspberries
2 egg whites	2 egg whites
100 g caster sugar	4 oz caster sugar
4 × 15 ml spoons water	4 tablespoons water
2 × 15 ml spoons lemon juice	2 tablespoons lemon juice
300 ml double cream	½ pint double cream

To finish:
Whipping cream
Whole raspberries or crystallised rose petals

To finish:
Whipping cream
Whole raspberries or crystallised rose petals

Especially delicious made with fresh raspberries, loganberries, strawberries or apricots, this is also very good made with any canned fruit except strawberries.

Sieve the raspberries. If using canned fruit strain off the juice, sieve the fruit, measure the purée and make up to 300 ml (½ pint) with some of the juice. Whisk the egg whites to stiff snow.

Put the sugar and water in a small saucepan and place over gentle heat. Stir until sugar has dissolved, then bring to the boil and cook rapidly without stirring until the syrup will form a thread (120°C, 250°F). Allow the syrup to stop bubbling, then pour slowly on to the beaten egg whites in a thin steady stream, holding the saucepan well above the basin and stirring continuously with a wooden spoon. When all the sugar is in, continue to beat until the mixture is thick and shiny and forms soft peaks. Stir in the fruit purée and lemon juice. Whip the cream into soft peaks and gradually fold in the fruit mixture. Sharpen to taste with lemon juice.

Pour into a mould or individual dariole tins and freeze. Remove Parfait from freezer into the refrigerator 1 hour before serving. Dip the mould briefly in hot water to unmould. Decorate with whipped cream and whole raspberries or crystallised rose petals. Serve with wafer biscuits or plain petits fours.

Iced melon sorbet

Metric	Imperial
1 small honeydew melon	1 small honeydew melon
100 g caster sugar	4 oz caster sugar
1 lemon	1 lemon
1 egg white	1 egg white

To decorate:
150 ml whipping cream
4 Maraschino or glacé cherries
8 fresh mint leaves or angelica diamonds

To decorate:
¼ pint whipping cream
4 Maraschino or glacé cherries
8 fresh mint leaves or angelica diamonds

This is an ideally refreshing dessert to serve after a rich or highly-spiced main course, such as curry. It is a charming decorative sweet for a dinner party.

Cut the melon in half lengthwise, discard the pips and scoop out the flesh. Put this in a blender with the sugar and 2 × 15 ml spoons (2 tablespoons) of lemon juice. Whisk until the sugar is dissolved. Pour into a freezer container and freeze until mushy.

Meanwhile cut the two pieces of melon shell in half lengthwise. Reform each into original shape, using two bowls of matching size lined with kitchen foil. Chill in refrigerator.

When the melon mixture is mushy turn into a bowl and whisk. Whisk egg white until stiff and fold into melon mixture; sharpen to taste with lemon juice. Pour into two melon shells, cover with foil and freeze. About 1 hour before required separate into four sections using a knife dipped into hot water. Place wedges on four dessert plates. Using a rose nozzle, pipe a zig-zag of whipped cream along the top of each wedge. Place a cherry in the centre with a frosted mint or angelica leaf on either side. Return to refrigerator until serving.

If you cannot get a small melon for 4 servings, use half a large one and cut it into 4 wedges.

Iced raspberry parfait; Iced melon sorbet

Chocolate ripple pears

Metric	Imperial
100 g plain chocolate	4 oz plain chocolate
3 × 15 ml spoons golden syrup	3 tablespoons golden syrup
75 ml single cream	3 fl oz single cream
4 ripe dessert pears	4 ripe dessert pears
1 family block vanilla and chocolate ice-cream	1 family block vanilla and chocolate ice-cream
25 g ratafia biscuits	1 oz ratafia biscuits

For maximum effect pour the rich Chocolate Sauce hot over the ice-cream and pears. But the sauce is also very good cold, and freezes well

First make the Chocolate Cream Sauce. Break up the chocolate and melt in a bowl over hot water. Blend in golden syrup. Heat the cream, without boiling, and gradually stir into the chocolate mixture. Keep warm over the hot water. (If serving cold, remove from heat and stir occasionally until chilled.)

Core, halve and peel the pears. Put two scoops of vanilla and chocolate ice-cream in each dessert dish and arrange a half pear on either side. Pour over the hot Chocolate Cream Sauce and garnish with ratafia biscuits, either whole or crushed.

Fire and ice

Metric	Imperial
4 medium Bramley apples	4 medium Bramley apples
25 g butter or margarine	1 oz butter or margarine
4 × 15 ml spoons demerara sugar	4 tablespoons demerara sugar
About 75 ml cider or water	About 3 fl oz cider or water
1 family block vanilla ice-cream	1 family block vanilla ice-cream
4 shelled walnuts or crushed gingernuts	4 shelled walnuts or crushed gingernuts

Cooking Time: 30–40 minutes
Oven: 190°C, 375°F, Gas Mark 5

The contrast of hot sharp-tasting roast apple with an ice-cold sweet topping makes exciting eating.

Wipe and core the apples. With a sharp knife, slit the skin round the 'equator'. Place the apples in a well-buttered fireproof dish and fill their centres with demerara sugar. Add sufficient cider or water to cover base of baking dish. Cover with a buttered sheet of greaseproof paper or foil. Bake in a preheated moderately hot oven for 30 minutes until tender – test with a skewer and do not overcook. Remove from oven, lift skin carefully off the apples and place in individual dishes.

Keep the apples warm while you boil the liquid in the base of the dish briskly until reduced to a syrupy consistency. Pour over the apples. Top each apple with a generous helping of ice-cream and a shelled walnut or crushed gingernut. Serve immediately.

Pineapple igloos

Metric	Imperial
3 egg whites	3 egg whites
175 g caster sugar	6 oz caster sugar
4 pineapple slices	4 pineapple slices
600 ml strawberry ice-cream	1 pint strawberry ice-cream
To garnish:	To garnish:
Glacé cherries	Glacé cherries
Angelica leaves	Angelica leaves
Caster sugar	Caster sugar

Cooking Time: 4–5 minutes
Oven: 230°C, 450°F, Gas Mark 8

This is a version of Baked Alaska made in individual portions with pineapple instead of sponge cake for the base. Use bought ice-cream or the Strawberry Parfait (see page 72).

Preheat the oven and place a shelf near the top. Whisk the egg whites until very stiff and dry. Sieve in 4 tablespoons sugar and continue whisking until stiff and shiny. Fold in the remaining sugar.

Place the pineapple slices on 4 ovenproof glass dishes. Pile the ice-cream evenly on top so that it does not project over the edge. Swirl the meringue over each one, covering the ice-cream and pineapple completely. Be careful to seal the edges right on to the plates or the ice-cream will melt and leak.

Decorate with glacé cherries and angelica and dredge with caster sugar. Put the dishes on a baking sheet and bake on top shelf of the preheated oven for 4–5 minutes, until delicately coloured and crisp. Serve at once.

Fire and ice; Chocolate ripple pears; Pineapple igloos

Apricot rum baba

Apricot rum baba

Metric	Imperial
125 g plain flour	4 oz plain flour
¼ teaspoon salt	¼ teaspoon salt
10 g fresh yeast ; or	¼ oz fresh yeast ; or
1½ × 5 ml spoons dried	1½ teaspoons dried
2 × 15 ml spoons caster sugar	2 tablespoons caster sugar
50 ml warm milk	2 fl oz warm milk
2 eggs, beaten	2 eggs, beaten
65 g butter, creamed	2½ oz butter, creamed

For the rum syrup:	For the rum syrup :
100 g caster sugar	4 oz caster sugar
175 ml water	6 fl oz water
100 ml rum	4 fl oz rum

For the decoration and filling:	For the decoration and filling :
Apricot glaze (see page 88)	Apricot glaze (see page 88)
225 g apricots, fresh or canned	8 oz apricots, fresh or canned
Angelica	Angelica
150 ml double cream	¼ pint double cream

Cooking Time: 40 minutes
Oven: 200°C, 400°F, Gas Mark 6;
    180°C, 350°F, Gas Mark 4

This is a lovely party sweet. In summer you can use strawberries, and Kirsch instead of rum in the syrup.

Sieve flour and salt into a bowl and put to warm. Cream the yeast with the sugar, add the warm milk and beaten eggs. Gradually stir into the flour and beat to a smooth batter. Cover the bowl with a clean cloth and leave in a warm place to prove for about 45 minutes or until the dough has doubled in bulk. Beat in the butter gradually. Half fill a greased 18 cm (7 in) Baba ring and leave in warm place until the dough rises to the rim.

Bake in a preheated moderately hot oven for 10 minutes, then reduce to moderate and continue cooking for 30 minutes or until a skewer inserted comes out clean. Remove from oven. Allow to shrink for 5–10 minutes, loosen with a knife and turn out on to a shallow pie dish, upside down.

Dissolve the sugar in the water, then boil fast until reduced to a syrup. Cool slightly and add the rum. Prick the Baba and spoon over the syrup. Baste frequently until all the syrup is absorbed.

Coat the Baba with Apricot Glaze. Arrange 8 apricot halves on the top and brush with glaze. Cut the angelica into leaves and insert between apricots. Cut up remaining apricots, fold into the whipped cream and pile into the centre of the Baba.

Mandarin charlotte russe

Mandarin charlotte russe

Metric

312 g can mandarin
oranges
135 g packet lemon jelly
15 g angelica
18 Boudoir biscuits
300 ml whipping cream
1–2 × 15 ml spoons Orange
Curaçao or Cointreau
(optional)

Imperial

11 oz can mandarin
oranges
4¾ oz packet lemon jelly
½ oz angelica
18 Boudoir biscuits
½ pint whipping cream
1–2 tablespoons Orange
Curaçao or Cointreau
(optional)

You can make this sweet the day before the party. In summer fill it with fresh raspberries or strawberries.
Rinse a 600 ml (1 pint) Charlotte mould with cold water. Drain the fruit. Dissolve the jelly thoroughly in 300 ml (½ pint) boiling water and add the fruit syrup making the liquid up to 450 ml (17 fl oz) with water if necessary.
Pour a thin layer of liquid jelly into the bottom of the mould and put in refrigerator to set.
Cut off one rounded end of the Boudoir biscuits so they are 1·5 cm (½ in) shorter than the sides of the mould.
When the first layer of jelly is set, arrange some of the mandarin sections on it in an attractive pattern with angelica diamonds, dipping each piece in liquid jelly before you put it in place. Refrigerate until set. When the pattern is firm cover with another layer of jelly and refrigerate. Meanwhile whip the cream until fairly stiff and fold in the liqueur if using.
When the jelly in the mould is firm dip the sugared side of the biscuits one at a time in liquid jelly and stand them closely together all round the sides of the mould, sugar side out. Fill the centre with alternate layers of cream and mandarin sections, ending with cream.
Slowly spoon remaining jelly down sides of mould between the biscuits, which will gradually absorb it. When jelly shows at the rim of the mould, chill Charlotte until required. Unmould and decorate with remaining cream and extra fruit if desired.

Summer rose meringue

Metric

For the Swiss Meringue:
225 g icing sugar, sieved
4 egg whites
¼ teaspoon vanilla essence
For the filling:
150 ml double cream
1–2 tablespoons Kirsch or
sherry
2 × 5 ml spoons caster
sugar
225 g loganberries,
raspberries or wild
strawberries
15 g crystallised rose petals

Imperial

For the Swiss Meringue:
8 oz icing sugar, sieved
4 egg whites
¼ teaspoon vanilla essence
For the filling:
¼ pint double cream
1–2 tablespoons Kirsch or
sherry
2 teaspoons caster
sugar
8 oz loganberries,
raspberries or wild
strawberries
½ oz crystallised rose petals

Cooking Time: 80 minutes
Oven: 140°C, 275°F, Gas Mark 1

One of the advantages of this pretty dessert is that you can make the meringue baskets when convenient and store them in an airtight container or in the freezer until required. It takes only a few minutes to fill them so they are very practical for a buffet party; wild strawberries would make them a super treat. The recipe makes 6.

Put the egg whites and icing sugar in a bowl over a saucepan of simmering water and follow the recipe for Swiss Meringue (page 89). Flavour with vanilla essence. Line 2 baking sheets with non-stick parchment or grease-proof paper and draw 18 circles 7 cm (3 in). If using greaseproof paper, oil lightly. Put the meringue mixture in a forcing bag with a large rose nozzle. Pipe rings just inside the circles. Fill in 6 rings with more meringue to make flat discs. Bake in preheated slow oven for 45 minutes or until crisp and delicately coloured. Remove from oven, cool and loosen meringue.

Mount 2 meringue rings on each disc, sticking them together with remaining meringue mixture. Return to oven for 20 minutes until firm. Remove and cool. Whip cream until stiff, fold in Kirsch or sherry and sugar to taste. Fold in prepared berries, pile into baskets and decorate with crystallised rose petals. For buffets serve baskets in paper meringue cases.

Chocolate, rum and raisin cheesecake

Chocolate, rum and raisin cheesecake

Metric	Imperial
150 g digestive biscuits	5 oz digestive biscuits
75 g butter	3 oz butter
50 g demerara sugar	2 oz demerara sugar
For the filling:	For the filling:
40 g raisins	1½ oz raisins
25 ml rum	1 fl oz rum
2 eggs, separated	2 eggs, separated
50 g caster sugar	2 oz caster sugar
1 × 5 ml spoon instant coffee	1 teaspoon instant coffee
5 x 15 ml spoons boiling water	5 tablespoons boiling water
12 g (1 envelope) powdered gelatine	½ oz (1 envelope) powdered gelatine
50 g plain chocolate	2 oz plain chocolate
225 g cream cheese	8 oz cream cheese
150 ml double cream	¼ pint double cream
2 × 15 ml spoons milk	2 tablespoons milk
To decorate:	To decorate:
150 ml double cream	¼ pint double cream
Chocolate flakes or crystallised flowers and leaves	Chocolate flakes or crystallised flowers and leaves

Vary this by using sweet sherry instead of rum or omitting the raisins altogether and using a double quantity of chocolate. Serves 6–8.

Soak the raisins in rum, preferably overnight. Crush the biscuits between sheets of greaseproof paper until fine. Melt the butter and stir in the crumbs and sugar. Stir over gentle heat until well blended and press into a greased 23 cm (9 in) flan dish or tin with a loose base. Refrigerate to harden well.

Mix egg yolks, sugar and the coffee dissolved in 2 × 15 ml spoons (2 tablespoons) of the boiling water in the top of a double saucepan or in a bowl. Place over boiling water and stir steadily until the mixture clings to the back of the wooden spoon.

Dissolve gelatine thoroughly in 3 × 15 ml spoons (3 tablespoons) of boiling water, stir into the egg mixture and remove from heat. Melt the chocolate with a little water in a bowl over boiling water. Stir until smooth and blend into mixture.

Beat the cream cheese and when the chocolate mixture is cold, stir it gradually into the cream cheese. Whisk the cream with the milk to soft peaks and fold into the mixture. Whisk the egg whites until stiff but not brittle and fold into mixture. Stir in rum-soaked raisins. Pour into flan dish or tin and refrigerate until firmly set.

Decorate with piped whipped cream and chocolate flakes or crystallised flowers and leaves.

Syllabub; Marrons Mont Blanc

Syllabub

Metric

1 lemon
100 ml medium white wine
3–4 × 15 ml spoons caster sugar
300 ml double cream

To decorate:
Chopped pistachio nuts or crushed praline (see page 66)

Imperial

1 lemon
4 fl oz medium white wine
3–4 tablespoons caster sugar
½ pint double cream

To decorate:
Chopped pistachio nuts or crushed praline (see page 66)

Light and quickly prepared, this dessert is for immediate serving, or can be kept overnight in the refrigerator.
Grate the rind delicately off the lemon so there is no trace of pith. Put it in a bowl with the strained lemon juice, wine and 3 × 15 ml spoons (3 tablespoons) sugar. (You can leave this mixture to infuse if there is time.) Strain out the lemon rind just before using.
Gradually add the cream, whisking steadily until the mixture stands in peaks. Taste and add more sugar if desired; this will depend on the wine you have used.
Pour the Syllabub into goblets or custard cups, swirling it up the centre, and chill thoroughly.
Decorate with chopped pistachio nuts or crushed praline and serve with French Tuile Biscuits.

Marrons Mont Blanc

Metric

50 g unsalted butter
25 g caster sugar
225 g can purée of marrons glacés
1–2 × 15 ml spoons sherry
Lemon juice to taste
150 ml double cream

To decorate:
Ratafia biscuits or miniature meringues

Imperial

2 oz unsalted butter
1 oz caster sugar
8 oz can purée of marrons glacés
1–2 tablespoons sherry
Lemon juice to taste
¼ pint double cream

To decorate:
Ratafia biscuits or miniature meringues

These little mounds of chestnut purée, topped with whipped cream like the snow-capped mountain from which they take their name, are one of the most delicious of all desserts.
Cream together the butter and sugar. Stir the chestnut purée in the tin and add it gradually to the creamed mixture. Flavour to taste with sherry and lemon juice, stirring it in gradually to avoid curdling.
Pile the chestnut purée into the centre of individual dessert dishes. Whip the cream and swirl on to the top of each little mound. Arrange ratafia biscuits or minature meringues round the base. Chill until required.

Jersey jumbles; Country jam pudding

Country jam pudding

Metric	Imperial
175 g self-raising flour	6 oz self-raising flour
40 g caster sugar	1½ oz caster sugar
50 g butter or margarine	2 oz butter or margarine
1 egg, beaten	1 egg, beaten
3–4 × 15 ml spoons jam, lemon curd or mincemeat	3–4 tablespoons jam, lemon curd or mincemeat

Cooking Time: 15–20 minutes
Oven: 200°C, 400°F, Gas Mark 6

A simple, quick pudding to make which can be eaten hot or cold and packs well for picnics.
Mix the flour and sugar together. Rub in the fat with the tips of the fingers until the consistency of breadcrumbs. Mix into a stiff dough with the egg and a little water. Knead lightly and divide in half. Roll out thinly into 2 rectangles of the same size. Place one on a greased baking sheet, prick and spread with preserve, leaving a margin round the edge. Brush the margin with water and place the second rectangle on top. Press the edges together and pinch with finger and thumb into flutes. Prick the top in a pattern with a fork. Bake in a preheated moderately hot oven for 15–20 minutes until risen and golden brown. Remove from oven, sprinkle with caster sugar and cut into squares. Serve hot with custard or cold with cream.

Jersey jumbles

Metric	Imperial
125 g plain flour	4 oz plain flour
Pinch of salt	Pinch of salt
1 × 5 ml spoon baking powder	1 teaspoon baking powder
Pinch of ground ginger	Pinch of ground ginger
Pinch of ground nutmeg	Pinch of ground nutmeg
25 g butter or margarine	1 oz butter or margarine
25 g caster sugar	1 oz caster sugar
1 egg, beaten	1 egg, beaten
Deep fat for frying	Deep fat for frying
Caster sugar for dredging	Caster sugar for dredging
Honey or syrup	Honey or syrup

Sieve the flour, salt, baking powder and spices into a basin. Rub in the fat with the finger tips. Mix in the sugar. Stir in the egg, adding a little water if necessary; the dough should be fairly stiff. Roll out on a floured board until about 1·5 cm (½ in) thick. Cut into 7 cm (3 in) rounds. With a smaller cutter, remove the centres to leave rings. Work up remaining dough, roll out and cut into strips 7 × 2·5 cm (3 × 1 in). Shape into twists.
Heat the fat to 190°C, 375°F; test by dropping in a piece of dough which should rise at once and start to swell. Drain the jumbles on soft paper and dredge with sugar. Serve with warmed honey or syrup.

Zabaglione

Metric	Imperial
3 egg yolks	3 egg yolks
75 g caster sugar	3 oz caster sugar
1 × 5 ml spoon finely grated lemon rind	1 teaspoon finely grated lemon rind
150 ml medium white wine or Marsala	¼ pint medium white wine or Marsala

This delicious wine whip can be served hot or cold, either as a light dessert or as a sweet sauce with hot sponge puddings or fruit compotes.

Whisk the egg yolks with the sugar and lemon rind until white, then whisk in the wine. Place the bowl over a saucepan of simmering water and continue whisking until the mixture thickens and falls in ribbons from the whisk. Pour into large wineglasses and serve at once as the mixture is likely to fall. Serve with sweet biscuits.

Cold zabaglione

Metric	Imperial
6 egg yolks	6 egg yolks
75 g caster sugar	3 oz caster sugar
Finely grated rind of 1 orange	Finely grated rind of 1 orange
150 ml Marsala or white wine	¼ pint Marsala or white wine
50 ml double cream	2 fl oz double cream
Chopped pistachio nuts or orange peel	Chopped pistachio nuts or orange peel

Follow the method for making hot Zabaglione and when the mixture has thickened to ribbon consistency, remove from heat, place in a bowl of iced water and continue whisking until cold. Very lightly whisk the cream with a fork and fold into the mixture. Pour into goblets and chill in refrigerator until required. Decorate with chopped pistachio nuts or fine twists of orange peel and serve with sweet finger biscuits. Alternatively pour over sliced fresh peaches, strawberries or fresh fruit salad.

Atholl brose

Metric	Imperial
4 × 15 ml spoons medium oatmeal or ground almonds	4 tablespoons medium oatmeal or ground almonds
3–4 × 15 ml spoons whisky	3–4 tablespoons whisky
1 × 15 ml spoon lemon juice	1 tablespoon lemon juice
2 × 15 ml spoons heather honey	2 tablespoons heather honey
150 ml double cream	¼ pint double cream
To decorate:	To decorate:
Twists of fresh lemon	Twists of fresh lemon

The Highland version of Syllabub, this is much better made with toasted oatmeal rather than with ground almonds. The amount of honey can be adjusted to taste. Spread the oatmeal on a tin and toast for a few minutes under the grill, shaking frequently so that it browns evenly. Leave to cool.

Mix together the whisky, lemon juice and honey. Gradually whisk in the cream until the mixture stands in soft peaks. Fold in the toasted oatmeal and turn into goblets. Chill until required. Decorate each goblet with a lemon twist and serve with thin shortbread biscuits.

Peppermint chocolate pears

Metric	Imperial
10–12 mint chocolate creams	10–12 mint chocolate creams
4 ripe Comice pears	4 ripe Comice pears
50 g crystallised ginger or glacé cherries, chopped	2 oz crystallised ginger or glacé cherries, chopped
150 ml single cream	¼ pint single cream
25 g walnuts, chopped	1 oz walnuts, chopped

This is a good party sweet for the youngsters and one they can easily make for themselves.

Cut up the chocolate mints and put them in a bowl over a saucepan of simmering water to melt.

Core pears from the bottom, leaving top with stalk intact. Peel and slice a sliver off the base so that pears will stand upright. Stuff with chopped ginger or cherries and place each pear in a small dessert dish.

Heat the cream, without boiling and add to the peppermint cream. Stir until smooth and pour over the pears. Sprinkle with chopped walnuts and serve at once.

Zabaglione; Atholl brose; Cold zabaglione; Peppermint chocolate pears

Belgian fruit flan

Metric

20 cm flan case of sweet shortcrust pastry (see page 50)

300 ml Pâtisserie Cream, vanilla flavour (see page 92)

125 g green or black grapes

2 large bananas

Juice of ½ lemon

125 g Apricot Glaze

For the Apricot glaze

125 g apricot jam

1 × 15 ml spoon lemon juice

Imperial

8 in flan case of sweet shortcrust pastry (see page 50)

½ pint Pâtisserie Cream, vanilla flavour (see page 92)

4 oz green or black grapes

2 large bananas

Juice of ½ lemon

4 oz Apricot Glaze

For the Apricot glaze

4 oz apricot jam

1 tablespoon lemon juice

You can vary the filling for this flan by choosing any fresh or canned fruit available. Use a redcurrant glaze for red berries or cherries and golden apricot glaze for other fruit. Serve the flan the day it is filled or the pastry will lose its crispness, but the flan case can be baked in advance and stored in a tin.

First make the vanilla-flavoured Pâtisserie Cream and leave it to cool, stirring continuously to prevent a skin forming. Meanwhile slit the grapes down one side and remove the pips. Peel and slice the bananas and pour over the lemon juice to prevent discoloration.

When the Pâtisserie Cream is cold spread it in the flan case. Arrange the fruit on top in an attractive pattern. Make the Apricot Glaze by dissolving apricot jam with a little lemon juice over a low heat. Spoon carefully over the fruit. To give the flan a professional finish brush the glaze over the top edges of the pastry.

Variation

Raspberry, strawberry or cherry flan

Prepare 450 g (1 lb) of fresh raspberries, hulled strawberries or stoned cherries. Flavour the Pâtisserie Cream with lemon juice and coat with Redcurrant Glaze.

Bavarian prune and apricot torte; Italian frangipane flan

Italian frangipane flan

Metric

20 cm flan case of sweet
shortcrust pastry (page 50)
70 g unsalted butter
40 g plain flour
1 whole egg plus one yolk
25 g caster sugar
150 ml milk
2 × 5 ml spoons finely
grated lemon rind
25 g ratafias or macaroons
1 × 15 ml spoon rum
¼ teaspoon vanilla essence
raspberry jam

Imperial

8 in flan case of sweet
shortcrust pastry (page 50)
2½ oz unsalted butter
1½ oz plain flour
1 whole egg plus one yolk
1 oz caster sugar
¼ pint milk
2 teaspoons finely grated
lemon rind
1 oz ratafias or macaroons
1 tablespoon rum
¼ teaspoon vanilla essence
raspberry jam

Melt 40 g (1½ oz) of the butter in a small saucepan.
Remove from heat and blend in the flour. Beat the eggs
and stir in gradually. Add the sugar and blend in the
milk. Replace the pan on the burner and heat gently,
stirring continuously until the mixture thickens and
begins to leave the sides of the pan. Remove from fire
and stir in the grated lemon rind, crushed ratafias, rum
and vanilla essence. Heat the remaining butter in a small
pan until it turns nut brown, then stir it into the cream
mixture to give it the characteristic frangipane flavour.
Spread the bottom of the flan case with jam. Pour in the
frangipane cream and smooth the top.
When cold decorate with rosettes of piped whipped
cream and halved or chopped pistachio kernels.

Bavarian prune and apricot torte

Metric

250 g plain flour
125 g unsalted butter
125 g caster sugar
3 egg yolks, beaten
¼ teaspoon vanilla essence
75 ml water

For the topping:
100 g prunes, soaked
50 g apricots, soaked
2–3 × 15 ml spoons lemon
juice
Caster sugar for dredging

Imperial

9 oz plain flour
4½ oz unsalted butter
4½ oz caster sugar
3 egg yolks, beaten
¼ teaspoon vanilla essence
3 fl oz water

For the topping:
4 oz prunes, soaked
2 oz apricots, soaked
2–3 tablespoons lemon
juice
Caster sugar for dredging

Cooking Time: 25 minutes
Oven: 200°C, 400°F, Gas Mark 6;
    180°C, 350°F, Gas Mark 4

Sieve the flour and rub in the butter with finger tips. Mix
in the sugar. Beat egg yolks with vanilla essence and
water and stir into dry ingredients. Add a little water
if necessary to give a soft dough. Knead lightly on a
floured board; pat out into a circle 6 mm (¼ in) thick and
place in a greased 20 cm (8 in) sandwich tin. Chill for
30 minutes. Stone prunes and arrange on top of the torte
with the apricots. Sprinkle with lemon juice and caster
sugar. Bake in a preheated hot oven for 15 minutes,
reduce heat and cook for 10 minutes or until golden and
set. Serve hot or cold with cream.

Gâteau St Honoré

Metric

For the choux pastry:
40 g butter or margarine
150 ml water
75 g plain flour, sieved
2 eggs, beaten

For the gâteau:
100 g sweet shortcrust
(see page 50)
300 ml Pâtisserie Cream
(see above) ; or 300 ml
Chantilly Cream (see page
23)
Rum or vanilla essence to
taste
75 g caster sugar

To decorate:
Crystallised rose and
violet petals

Imperial

For the choux pastry:
1½ oz butter or margarine
¼ pint water
3 oz plain flour, sieved
2 eggs, beaten

For the gâteau:
4 oz sweet shortcrust
(see page 50)
½ pint Pâtisserie Cream
(see above) ; or ½ pint
Chantilly Cream (see page
23)
Rum or vanilla essence to
taste
3 oz caster sugar

To decorate:
Crystallised rose and
violet petals

Cooking Time : 35 minutes
Oven : 220°C, 425°F, Gas Mark 7 ;
190°C, 375°F, Gas Mark 5

In France this is often used as a birthday party dessert. For children the candles can be inserted in the little choux puffs which are coated with caramel or chocolate glacé icing.

Melt the butter in the water, bring to the boil and tip in the flour. Beat until smooth over gentle heat until the dough leaves the sides of the pan. Cool and beat in the eggs very gradually, 1 × 15 ml spoon (1 tablespoon) at a time. If you do this too quickly the dough will be too soft to pipe.

Roll out the sweet shortcrust into a round about 20 cm (8 in) across. Place on a greased baking sheet and prick well. Damp the outside edge of the round. With a forcing bag and a 1·5 cm/½ in plain nozzle pipe a ring of choux pastry on top of the damp edge.

Pipe the rest of the choux pastry in small 'buns' the same width as the ring, on another greased baking sheet. Place shortcrust base on a shelf near the top of preheated oven, with small puffs below it. Bake for 15 minutes and reduce heat, reverse baking trays. Cook for a further 20 minutes. Remove from oven and cool pastry. Slit choux ring and puffs to allow steam to escape.

Flavour Pâtisserie Cream or Chantilly Cream with rum or vanilla. When cold, fill puffs.

Heat the caster sugar in small thick saucepan over gentle heat until it turns golden. Dip base of puffs in caramel and fix on ring. Trickle remaining caramel on top of puffs and quickly decorate with crushed rose petals and violet petals alternately, before caramel sets. Pile remaining cream into centre of gateau and decorate top.

Pâtisserie cream

Metric

2 egg yolks
1 egg white
50 g caster sugar
25 g plain flour, sieved
300 ml milk
¼ teaspoon vanilla essence

Alternative flavourings:
Lemon juice, sweet sherry,
rum

Imperial

2 egg yolks
1 egg white
2 oz caster sugar
1 oz plain flour, sieved
½ pint milk
¼ teaspoon vanilla essence

Alternative flavourings:
Lemon juice, sweet sherry,
rum

Whisk the eggs and sugar together until nearly white. Gradually stir in the flour and then the milk. Pour into a small saucepan and bring to the boil, simmering steadily. Simmer for 3–5 minutes ; it will not curdle. Flavour to taste with vanilla, lemon, sherry or rum. Pour on to a cold plate to cool and stir occasionally to prevent a skin forming. Use as required.

Gâteau St. Honoré

Chocolate roulade

Chocolate roulade

Metric

6 eggs, separated
¼ teaspoon vanilla essence
225 g caster sugar
50 g cocoa

For the filling:
100 g plain chocolate
2 × 15 ml spoons water
450 ml Chantilly Cream
(see page 23) ; or double
cream, whipped

To decorate:
150 ml double cream
Crystallised violets or lilac
Mint leaves or angelica
diamonds

Imperial

6 eggs, separated
¼ teaspoon vanilla essence
8 oz caster sugar
2 oz cocoa

For the filling:
4 oz plain chocolate
2 tablespoons water
¾ pint Chantilly Cream
(see page 23) ; or double
cream, whipped

To decorate:
¼ pint double cream
Crystallised violets or lilac
Mint leaves or angelica
diamonds

Cooking Time: 20 minutes
Oven: 180°C, 350°F, Gas Mark 4

This is a luscious party pudding from France.
Line a 33 × 21 cm (13 × 8½ in) swiss roll tin with greased greaseproof paper (see page 30).
Whip egg yolks, vanilla essence and sugar until creamy. Sieve and fold in cocoa. Whisk egg whites until stiff but not brittle and fold into mixture. Pour into prepared tin and spread evenly into corners.
Bake in preheated oven for 20 minutes or until set and springy to the touch, but still soft. Do not overcook or it will crack when rolled up. Remove from oven, allow to shrink slightly and turn out upside down on greased greaseproof paper.
Break up chocolate and melt with the water in a bowl over a saucepan of simmering water. Stir until smooth and spread over cake. Cover with Chantilly Cream or whipped cream. Roll up like Swiss Roll (see page 31).
Remove to a serving platter and decorate with ribbons of piped whipped cream, crystallised flowers and mint leaves, angelica or nuts.
(Serves 8)

Glossary

ANGELICA: Herb with delicate muscatel flavour. Crystallised stems used to decorate cakes and desserts, or chopped and mixed with cake and pudding fruits.

BAIN MARIE: (French) a) Saucepan or baking dish standing in a large pan of simmering water either in oven or on hot plate. b) Double saucepan with water in lower container. A method of cooking or keeping food warm when it is liable to curdle if cooked quickly.

BAKING PARCHMENT: Silicone-treated lining material for baking tins which is non-stick and does not require greasing.

BAKING POWDER: Raising agent for flour consisting of 1 part cream of tartar to 2 parts bicarbonate of soda. When liquid is added a gas is released and forms bubbles which raise the dough during cooking.

BATTER: Mixture of flour, egg and milk or water used for coating food before frying or for making puddings and cakes which are fried or baked.

BICARBONATE OF SODA: A raising agent used for soda bread and sour milk scones, moist gingerbreads etc.

BLANCH: To scald fruit, almonds etc., in boiling water from 1–4 minutes so their skins can easily be removed.

CANDIED PEEL: Peel and pith of citrus fruits, usually orange lemon and citron, cooked, boiled in syrup and dried. Used chopped in cakes and puddings.

CARAMELISE: To boil sugar slowly until it turns into toffee consistency and becomes deep golden brown. Used for colouring, flavouring and glazing.

CANTALOUPE MELON: Round Musk Melon with rough skin and sweet orange-tinted flesh. Originally came from Cantaloupe, Italy.

CHAFING DISH: Frying pan used with a table cooker, usually a spirit lamp, for flamed desserts and quickly cooked dishes.

CINNAMON: Aromatic bark of a tropical tree sold in sticks, quills or ground. Used chiefly to spice cakes and puddings.

CITRON: Large lemon-shaped citrus fruit with very thick rind which has a fragrant flavour when crystallised and is used in cakes and puddings.

CLARIFIED BUTTER: Purified butter which has been heated and all suspended matter strained out, leaving pure fat for frying.

CREAM: (Fresh) Fat allowed to ride to top of milk and separated. Single Cream: 18% butter fat, will not whip or freeze. Whipping Cream: 38% butter fat, will whip, excellent for cold soufflés and pastry fillings. Double Cream: 48% butter fat, will whip and freeze. If whipped, must not be refrozen. Clotted Cream: Thick cream skimmed off cold scalded milk. Specialty of Devon and Cornwall; served with scones, sponges, puddings and fruit.

COINTREAU: Orange-flavoured liqueur.

COMPOTE: Fresh or diced fruit cooked in syrup.

CONDENSED MILK: Milk evaporated to thick viscous consistency, heavily sweetened and canned.

CURRANTS: (dried) Small Corinth grapes grown for drying.

DEMERARA SUGAR: Honey-coloured crystals of cane sugar.

DREDGE: To coat food with sugar or flour using a flour sifter or sugar caster.

EVAPORATED MILK: Canned milk evaporated by two thirds, unsweetened.

FLAMBÉ: (French) Food flamed with alcohol such as Brandy, Rum or liqueur, during cooking or at the end and served while still flaming.

GALETTE: A thin flat cake, usually of pastry.

GATEAU: A cake made of rich sponge or pastry, usually with creamy filling, iced and decorated.

GILL: 150 ml = ¼ pint (Imperial) = 5 fluid oz.

GLACÉ (French) Glazed with sugar syrup (fruit), or with icing sugar (cakes).

GLAZE: A shiny coating made with jam, jelly or egg white and sugar for sweet pastries, or with milk or egg yolk and water for breads.

GRAND MARNIER: Orange-flavoured liqueur.

GRIDDLE: Girdle in Scotland, Bakestone in Wales, is a thick iron plate used on top of the stove for cooking scones, pancakes etc.

HARD SAUCE: Creamed butter and sugar flavoured with brandy, rum or whisky and served chilled with hot puddings.

HONEYDEW MELON: Large oval melon, smooth skinned with sweet yellow/green flesh.

KIRSCH: White spirit distilled from wild black cherries.

LEMON CURD: Preserve made with lemon juice, eggs, butter and sugar used as filling for cakes and pastries.

MANDARIN: Citrus fruit with loose skin similar to tangerine in shape and flavour.

MAPLE SYRUP: Sap from maple tree boiled into syrup and refined. Served with waffles, pancakes and various American sweets.

MARASCHINO: Liqueur made from wild cherries of Central Europe. 'Maraschino cherries' are bottled in the liqueur and used for fillings, desserts, ice-creams etc.

MOCHA: Coffee blended with chocolate for cakes, puddings and ice cream.

ORANGE CURAÇAO: Orange-flavoured liqueur made from bitter oranges grown in Curaçao.

PASSION FRUIT: Tropical plum-sized fruit of the passion flower (granadillo) with wrinkled purple skin and fragrant juicy yellow pulp.

POTATO FLOUR: (Fécule) Finely milled potato starch used in delicate sponges and for thickening sauces.

PRALINE: Unblanched almonds cooked in caramelised sugar and crushed for serving with or garnishing cold sweets and gâteaux.

PURÉE: Raw or cooked fruit or other food, passed through a sieve or mashed in an electric blender.

RAISIN: Large white grapes, seeded or seedless, and sun dried.

RAMEKINS: Individual ovenproof dishes or small pastry cases.

RATAFIA BISCUITS: Tiny macaroons flavoured with almonds, used crushed in sweets or whole as garnish.

ROUX: (French) Butter and flour, usually in equal quantities, cooked together and used as a base to thicken sauces.

SAGO: Starch made from the pith of the sago palm, used to make milk puddings or thicken sauces and purées.

SCALD: To heat milk or cream until just below boiling point. To plunge fruits briefly into boiling water to facilitate peeling.

SHORTENING: Animal or vegetable fat which contains very little water and produces pastry with crisp 'short' texture.

SORBET: (French) Sherbet or water ice made with fruit juice.

SOURED CREAM: Cream soured by lactic acid used for sauces and salad dressings.

SPUN SUGAR: Sugar boiled to caramel stage, 380°F (190°C) cooled slightly and drawn into thin threads for decorating desserts and cakes.

STEAMER: Double saucepan with lower part for water and upper container perforated to allow steam through to cook food.

STEAM BAKE: To cook food in a bain-marie in the oven so that it remains moist during slow cooking.

SULTANA: Small dried seedless white grapes.

SYRUP: Sugar and water boiled together.

TAPIOCA: Starch granules made from the cassava plant which become transparent and gelatinous when cooked.

TEFLON: Non-stick plastic finish to cooking utensils.

TORTE: (German) Continental cake with ground nuts and bread crumbs and little or no flour.

TREACLE: (Molasses) Dark viscous by-product of sugar refining.

VANILLA POD: Seed pod of the vanilla orchid, dried and used for flavouring by infusing in milk or stored in a jar of caster sugar to make vanilla sugar. Pod should be split as seeds are particularly aromatic.

VERMICELLI: (Italian) Pasta drawn into thin threads finer than spaghetti.

YEAST: Leavening agent for dough made from brewers barm, drained and compressed; this is fresh yeast, a living organism killed by heat. Dried yeast is the processed form made into granules.

ZEST: Fine outer rind of citrus fruits which contains aromatic oil. Removed in thin slivers, avoiding pith, for infusing, or finely grated for flavouring or garnish.

Index